LET'S COOK KENYA

National Ethnic Foods

Susan Kamau

Published by Susan Kamau.
Sliced Onion Company Limited.
P. O. Box 41042 Nairobi,
00100 Kenya.

© 2013 Susan Kamau.

All rights reserved.

Be advised that the traditional recipes contained in this book have been given in good faith as a contribution to the common good and the furtherance of mutual understanding. This publication may not be reproduced in whole or part and in any form without special permission of the copyright holder provided due acknowledgement of the source is made. Reproduction for sale or other commercial purposes is prohibited without prior written permission from the copyright holder.

Design and Layout: Fozia Tariq.

Photographs (Cover & Food): David Beatty

Photographs (Kenya Landscapes): Michael Poliza

Photographs (Peoples of Kenya): National Museums of Kenya, Archives Section.

ISBN 978 9966 060 532

Printed by: English Press Limited. Enterprise Rd. P.O. Box 30127 Nairobi Kenya.

Acknowledgements

The production of any publication work involves an enormous number of people. I am grateful to all those involved in the production of this cook book.

My sincere appreciation goes to all respective contributors for their recipes:

INDIAN	Sharon Bedi	Nakuru Town
KAMBA	Salome Mbevi	Kyau Village, Makueni
BORANA	Wario Tadicha	Ola Village, Moyale
LUHYA	Muteshi Muhanji	Shinyalu Village, Kakamega (W)
LUO	Cheche Olweny	Kasimori Village, Kisumu Rural
BRITISH	Anne Jones	Karen, Nairobi
KIKUYU	Susan Njuguna	Kiambogo Village, Molo
KISII	Rebecca Kiago	Keroka, Kisii
KALENJIN	Atai Kapkara	Gituamba Village, Mt. Elgon
MAASAI	Steven Ganyagua	Oloosirkon Village, Kajiado (N)
MERU	Joyce Mutai	Uruku Village, South Imenti
MIJIKENDA	Maria Mwasambu	Dzastoni Village, Kilifi District
SOMALI	Adan Hussein	Bulapesa Village, Isolo
SOMALI	Hassan Adan	Baruwaqo Village, Wajir

Special Thanks to:

Susan's Makeup Artist	Wacuka Thimba
Susan's Hair Stylist	Corrine Muthoni Nyumoo
Susan's Dress	Leo Santana Fashions
Susan's Shoes	Instyle Shoez
Cover shot - styling	Wambui Thimba
Jewellery	Bij Crafts
Table accessories	Spinner's Web Ltd
Food Shoot Location	Leonard Mudachi
Researcher	Lydia Mbevi Nderitu
Archivist	Immelda Kithuka
Photographs (Cover & Food)	David Beatty
Photographs (Kenya Landscapes)	Michael Poliza
Photographs (Peoples of Kenya)	National Museums of Kenya
Layout & Design	Fozia Tariq
Printing	English Press Ltd

Contents

01	Acknowledgements
02	Contents
04	Introduction
05	Foreward
06	Linguistic communities of Kenya
11	**Borana**
14	Anshiri
16	Foon
18	Koche Balls
21	**British**
24	Fish & Chips
26	Toad in the Hole
28	Steak & Kidney Pie
31	**Indian**
34	Masala Chicken
36	Chilli Paneer Pasanda
38	Black Lentil Curry
41	**Kalenjin**
44	Mushebebit
46	Boinnet
48	Magrek
51	**Kamba**
54	Ngunza Kutu
56	Kinaa
58	Muthokoi
61	**Kikuyu**
64	Mukimo wa Miinji
66	Ngondu
68	Ucuru wa Kugagatia

71	**Kisii**
74	Obukima Bwobore
76	Omutwe we Mburi
78	Sagaa
80	Omugaye
83	**Luhya**
86	Tsiswa
88	Mrenda
90	Bilenje
92	Sikhinga
95	**Luo**
98	Aluru
100	Sukuma Osuga Mix
102	Oodol
104	Aliya
107	**Maasai**
110	Rongera
112	Ole Naotho
114	Mururi
117	**Meru**
120	Muree
122	Marigo
124	Njahi
126	Ruguru
129	**Mijikenda**
132	Muhogo
134	Mchele na kunde
136	Samaki wa Nazi
139	**Somali**
142	Somali Anjera
144	Birris
146	Basta
148	**Kenya Map**
150	**Index**

Introduction

Dedicated to my daughter, Martha and to Kenya's future generations.

This is a cookbook that I hope will draw the non-Kenyan and engage us, the locals. I got the urge to put the book together after the disputed general elections of 2007. My baby was 5 months old at that time as I watched coverage on the television of scenes of marooned mothers with tiny babies unable to move and feed them… burning and looting… I cried in front of my TV set, my heart bleeding and prayed to God. What madness was this?

I felt that the time was ripe for this book especially now with the 2013 general elections behind us. I want us never to forget the chaos that happened then and I want to show you that we may unite and love through our foods.

I'd like to encourage Kenyans to explore through their taste buds and to enjoy ethnic cooking and culture from across our communities. We must embrace our differences and love our diversity especially when it comes to our cuisines as this is truly our universal bonder.

Susan Kamau.

Foreward

Cooking shouldn't kill!

The Global Alliance for Clean Cookstoves is a public-private partnership led by the United Nations Foundation to save lives, improve livelihoods, empower women, and protect the environment by creating a thriving global market for clean and efficient household cooking solutions. Susan Kamau is a founding member of the Alliance Chef Corps, an international group of chefs dedicated to raising awareness about inefficient and dangerous cooking practices.

The Alliance's goal is for 100 million households to adopt clean cooking solutions by 2020. The Alliance is working with hundreds of public, private, and nonprofit partners to help overcome the market barriers that currently impede the production, deployment, and use of clean cookstoves and fuels in developing countries.

www.cleancookstoves.org

GLOBAL ALLIANCE FOR CLEAN COOKSTOVES

Linguistic classification of Kenyan Communities

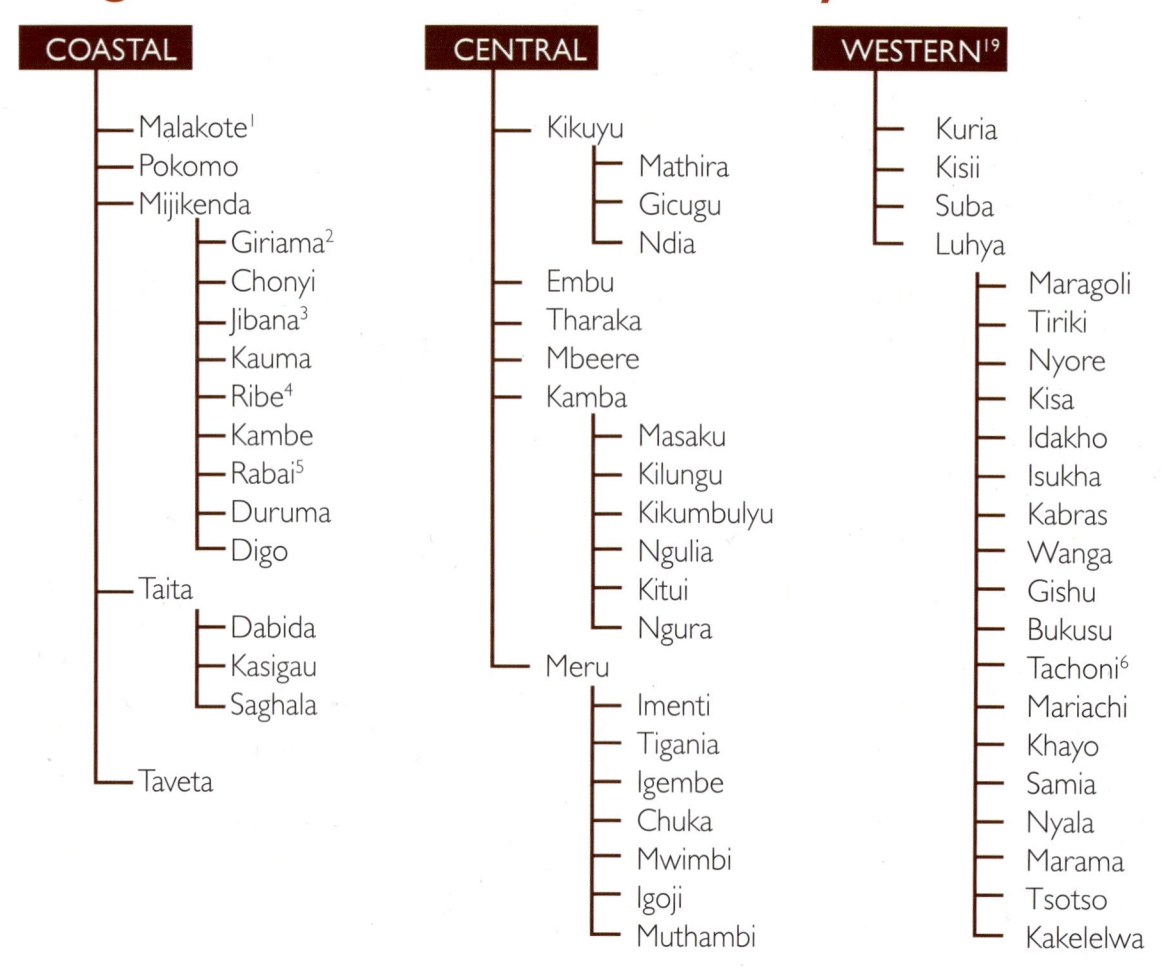

COASTAL
- Malakote[1]
- Pokomo
- Mijikenda
  - Giriama[2]
  - Chonyi
  - Jibana[3]
  - Kauma
  - Ribe[4]
  - Kambe
  - Rabai[5]
  - Duruma
  - Digo
- Taita
  - Dabida
  - Kasigau
  - Saghala
- Taveta

CENTRAL
- Kikuyu
  - Mathira
  - Gicugu
  - Ndia
- Embu
- Tharaka
- Mbeere
- Kamba
  - Masaku
  - Kilungu
  - Kikumbulyu
  - Ngulia
  - Kitui
  - Ngura
- Meru
  - Imenti
  - Tigania
  - Igembe
  - Chuka
  - Mwimbi
  - Igoji
  - Muthambi

WESTERN[19]
- Kuria
- Kisii
- Suba
- Luhya
  - Maragoli
  - Tiriki
  - Nyore
  - Kisa
  - Idakho
  - Isukha
  - Kabras
  - Wanga
  - Gishu
  - Bukusu
  - Tachoni[6]
  - Mariachi
  - Khayo
  - Samia
  - Nyala
  - Marama
  - Tsotso
  - Kakelelwa

Bantu

LAKE[20]	**HIGHLANDS**	**PLAINS**

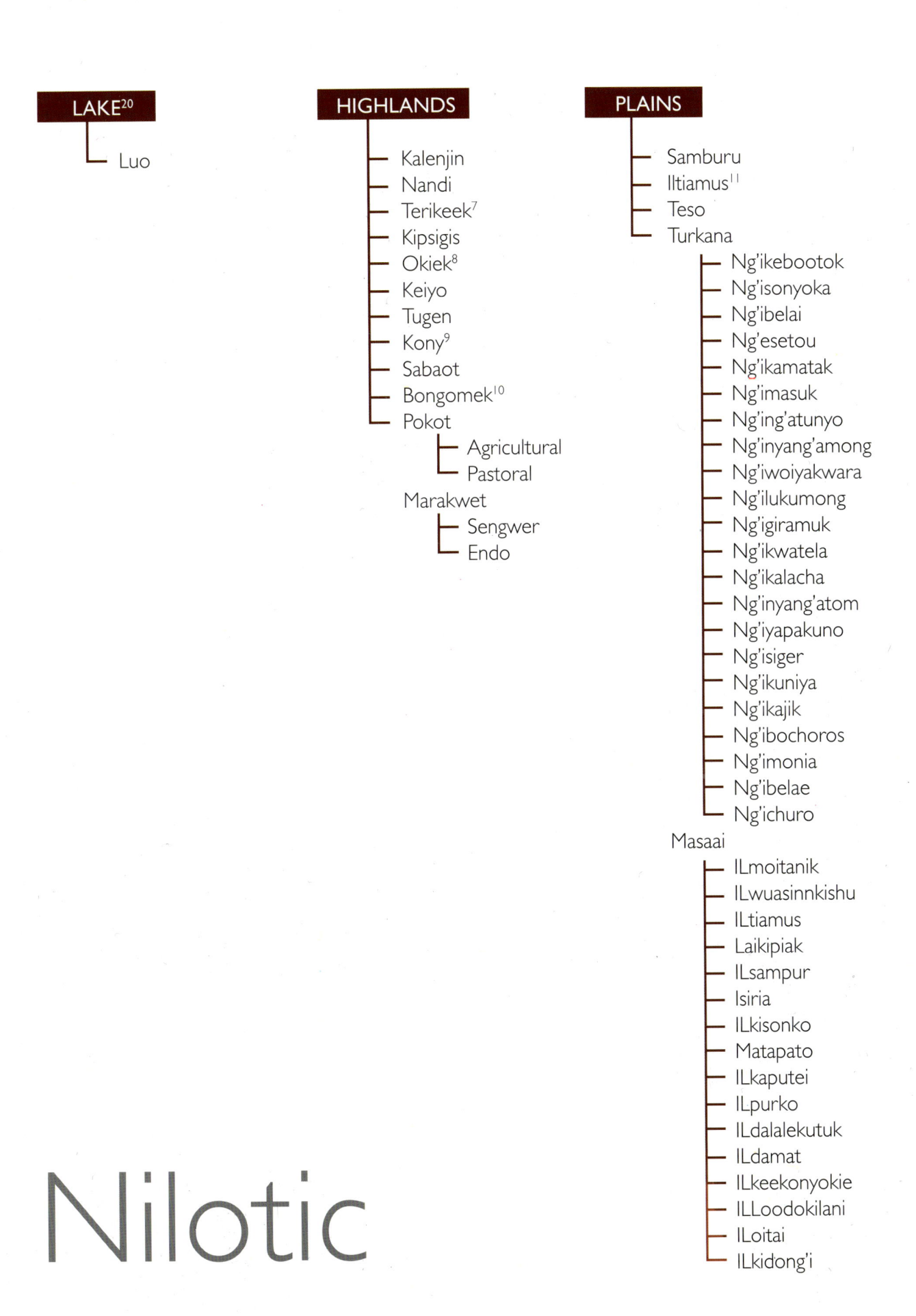

- Luo

- Kalenjin
- Nandi
- Terikeek[7]
- Kipsigis
- Okiek[8]
- Keiyo
- Tugen
- Kony[9]
- Sabaot
- Bongomek[10]
- Pokot
  - Agricultural
  - Pastoral
- Marakwet
  - Sengwer
  - Endo

- Samburu
- Iltiamus[11]
- Teso
- Turkana
  - Ng'ikebootok
  - Ng'isonyoka
  - Ng'ibelai
  - Ng'esetou
  - Ng'ikamatak
  - Ng'imasuk
  - Ng'ing'atunyo
  - Ng'inyang'among
  - Ng'iwoiyakwara
  - Ng'ilukumong
  - Ng'igiramuk
  - Ng'ikwatela
  - Ng'ikalacha
  - Ng'inyang'atom
  - Ng'iyapakuno
  - Ng'isiger
  - Ng'ikuniya
  - Ng'ikajik
  - Ng'ibochoros
  - Ng'imonia
  - Ng'ibelae
  - Ng'ichuro
- Masaai
  - ILmoitanik
  - ILwuasinnkishu
  - ILtiamus
  - Laikipiak
  - ILsampur
  - Isiria
  - ILkisonko
  - Matapato
  - ILkaputei
  - ILpurko
  - ILdalalekutuk
  - ILdamat
  - ILkeekonyokie
  - ILLoodokilani
  - ILoitai
  - ILkidong'i

Nilotic

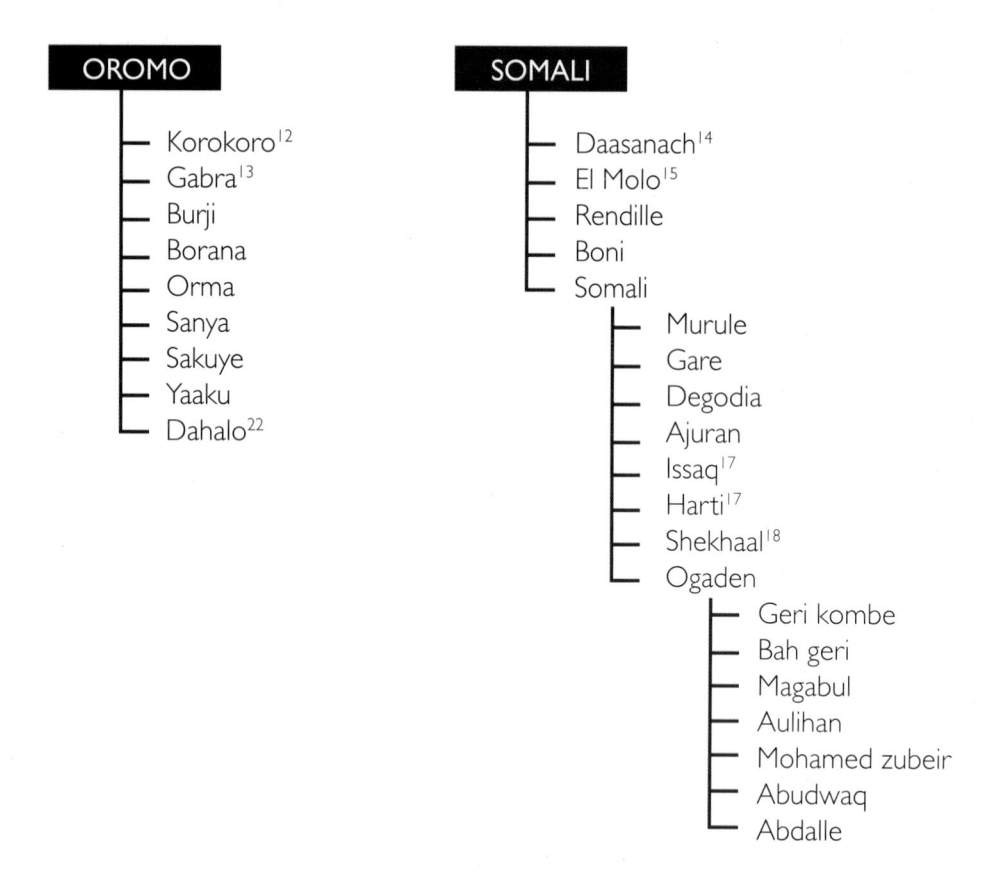

OROMO
- Korokoro[12]
- Gabra[13]
- Burji
- Borana
- Orma
- Sanya
- Sakuye
- Yaaku
- Dahalo[22]

SOMALI
- Daasanach[14]
- El Molo[15]
- Rendille
- Boni
- Somali
  - Murule
  - Gare
  - Degodia
  - Ajuran
  - Issaq[17]
  - Harti[17]
  - Shekhaal[18]
  - Ogaden
    - Geri kombe
    - Bah geri
    - Magabul
    - Aulihan
    - Mohamed zubeir
    - Abudwaq
    - Abdalle

Cushitic

MINORS

- Swahili[16]
  - Bajun
- Arabic
- Asian
- European
- Others

Key to the superscript numerals
1. Ilwana
2. Jiriama
3. Jihana
4. Rive
5. Rahai
6. Nandi x Maragoli
7. Terik = Nyang'ori
8. Also affiliated to Kisii and Masaai
9. Elgony (Kony), Sebei in Uganda
10. Pok or Pongomek
11. Njemps
12. Munyo
13. Linguistically not distinct from Borana
14. Ng'i-marille (by Turkana), Shangila (by Gabra/Borana) Gelba (by Rendille)
15. Classified as cushitic but now speak a dialect closely related to Samburu
16. Bantu (and others) x Arabic (and others)
17. Mainly in urban centres
18. Mainly religious and urban
19. Interlacustrine Bantu
20. River - Lake Nilotes
21. Divided into Southern and Eastern speakers. Both the Oromo and Somali divisions belong to the Eastern Cushitic speakers
22. The Dahalo, near the Tana river are the only southern Cushitic speakers in Kenya

Courtesy: "Traditional food plants of Kenya". Patrick Maundu, Kenya Resource Centre For Indigenous Knowledge, 1999.

Others

10

Borana

Anshiri 14
Foon 16
Koche Balls 18

Chalbi Desert.
Because water is scarce in the Chalbi Desert, the Borana regularly trek to springs in the eastern part of the desert with their camels. Sometimes there are up to 2,000 camels drinking at these springs after going many days without water. Algae give the water a greenish cast.

Burji man weaving

The Oromo are one of the Cushitic speaking groups of people with variations in colour and physical characteristics ranging from Hamitic to Nilotic. Although Oromos have their own unique culture, history, language, and civilization, they are culturally related to Afars, Somalis, Sidamas, Agaws, Bilens, Bejas, Kunamas, and other groups. In the past, Oromos had an egalitarian social system known as gada. Their military organization made them one of the strongest ethnic groups in the Horn of Africa between the twelfth and nineteenth centuries. Gada was a form of constitutional government and also a social system. Political leaders were elected by the men of the community every eight years. Corrupt or dictatorial leaders would be removed from power through buqisu (recall) before the official end of their term. Oromo women had a parallel institution known as siqqee. This institution promoted gender equality in Oromo society.

Oromos call their nation and country Oromia. They have been living in the Horn of Africa for all of their known history. The 3.5 million-year-old fossilized human skeleton known as "Lucy" (or "Chaltu" in Oromo) was found by archaeologists in Oromia. Present-day Oromos also live in Kenya and Somalia. Oromia is considered the richest region of the Horn of Africa because of its agricultural and natural resources. It is considered by many to be the "breadbasket" of the Horn. Farm products, including barley, wheat, sorghum, xafi (a grain), maize, coffee, oil seeds, chat (a stimulant leaf), oranges, and cattle are raised in abundance in Oromia. Oromia is also rich in gold, silver, platinum, marble, uranium, nickel, natural gas, and other mineral resources. It has several large and small rivers used for agriculture and for producing hydroelectric power.

The Oromo language is called Afaan Oromoo. Afaan Oromoo is the third most widely spoken language in Africa, after Arabic and Hausa. Original Oromo religion does not believe in hell and heaven. If a person commits a sin by disturbing the balance of nature or mistreating others, the society imposes punishment while the person is alive.

The main foods of Oromos are animal products including foon (meat), anan (milk), badu (cheese), dhadha (butter), and cereals that are eaten as marqa (porridge) and bideena (bread). Oromos drink coffee, dhadhi (honey wine), and faarso (beer). Some Oromos chew chat (a stimulant leaf). The majority of Oromos eat twice a day, in the morning and at night.

The Oromo are said to be of two major groups or moieties descended from the two 'houses' (wives) of the person Oromo represented by Borana and Barentu (Barenttuma). They include Borana, Macha, Tuuiiama, Wallo, Garrii, Gurraa, Arsi, Karrayyu, Itu, Ala, Qaiioo, Anniyya, Tummugga or Marawa, Orma, Akkichuu, Liban, Jile, Gofa, Sidamo, Sooddo, Galaan, Gujii and many others.

BORANA

Anshiri

Ingredients
5 cups dry maize kernels
salt to taste
fresh milk

Method
Use the large mortar and pestle (similar to the one used by the Kamba community).
Pound the dried maize to remove the outer skin.
Boil the maize until its tender.
Drain the water and pour in fresh milk.
Season with salt. Eaten like that as a meal.

Serves 3.

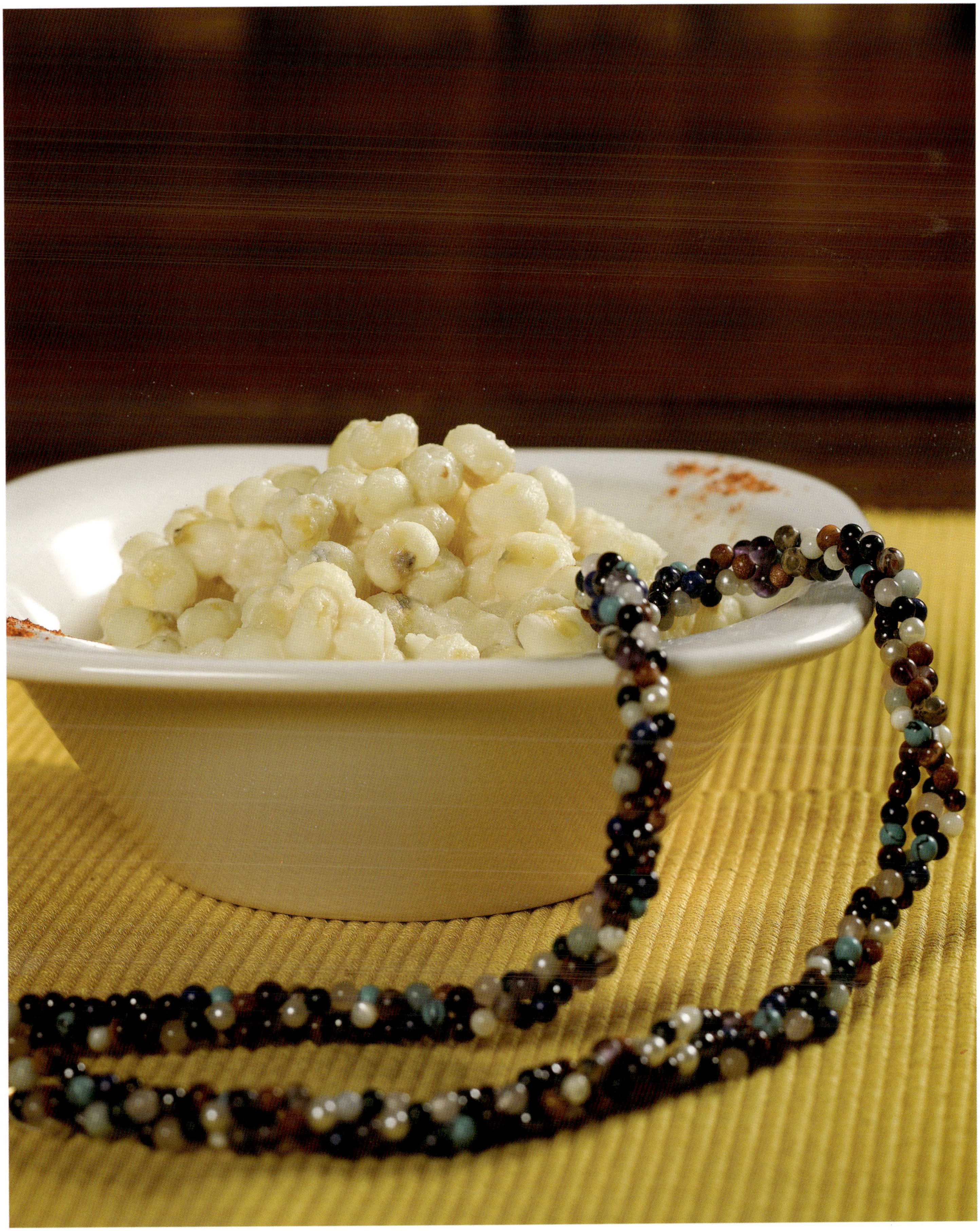

BORANA

Foon

Ingredients

1kg beef or chicken or mutton, diced
qara spice, to taste
1 onion, finely chopped
tomatoes, chopped
ginger, crushed

garlic, crushed
½ cup oil
salt to taste

Method

Fry the meat with a little oil and onion cut into very small pieces and fry until tender, sprinkle salt.
Add water and keep stirring until it's like porridge in terms of consistency.
Add tomatoes without their skin and crush them into this mixture.
Add qara spice, ginger and garlic and keep stirring.
Add oil and keep stirring until it is well mixed, sauce is deep red.
Ensure that there is enough water so that it does not stick to the pot.
Add a cooked boiled egg.
Eaten with injera bread.

Qara is dried red pepper ground into a fine powder combined with herbs and dried in a hot pot over fire.

Serves 4.

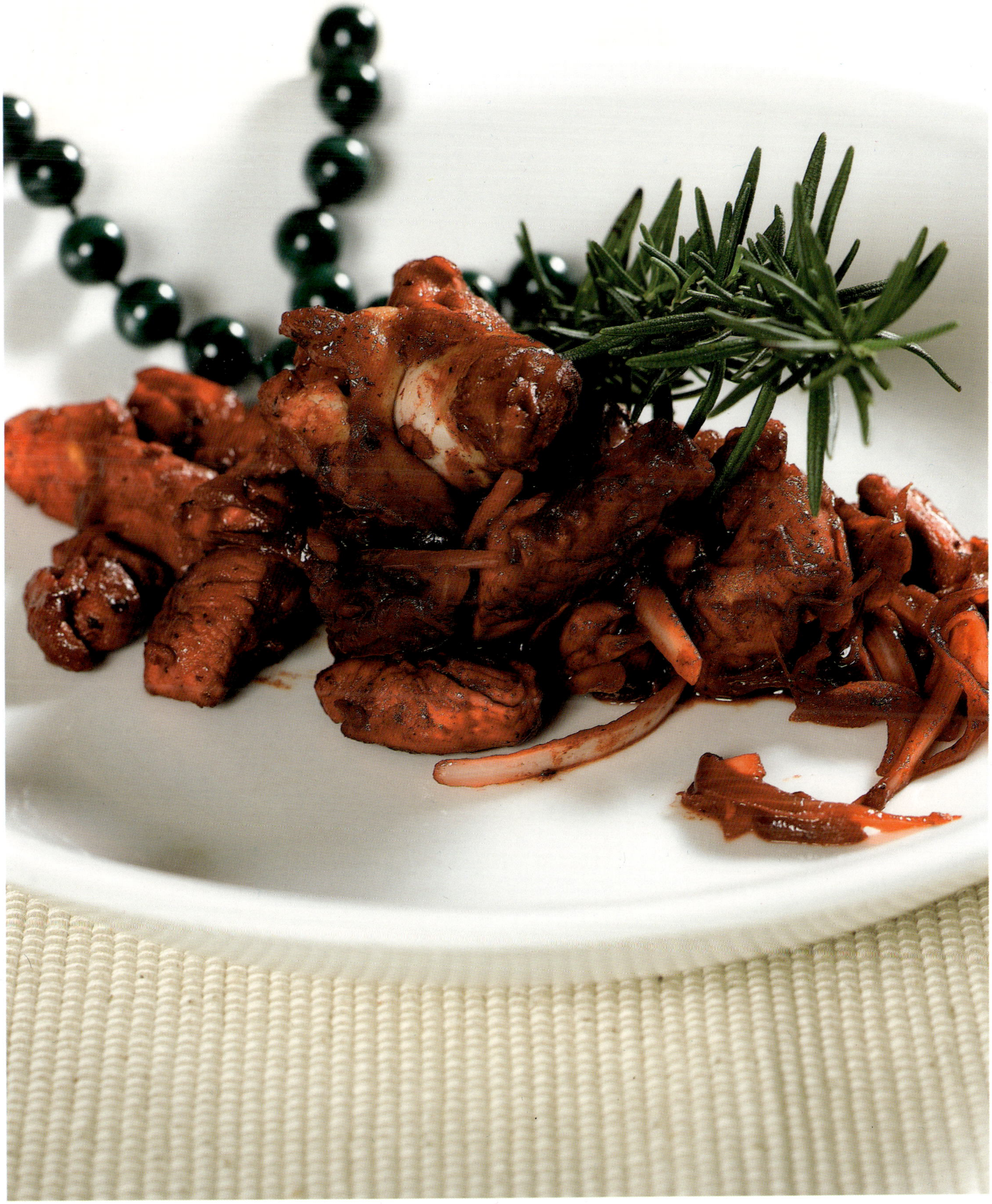

BORANA

Koche Balls

Ingredients

1kg beef, cubed
8 cups wheat flour
10 eggs
sugar
salt
milk
oil for deep frying

Method

Cut your beef steak into small cubes.
Fry with a little oil until it's cooked and begins to turn black.
Mix wheat flour with eggs and sugar and a little milk to get firm dough.
Add in the cooked meat.
Form the dough mixture into medium sized balls.
Heat oil in a pan.
Drop the balls into the pan and let them cook until golden brown.

Serves 3.

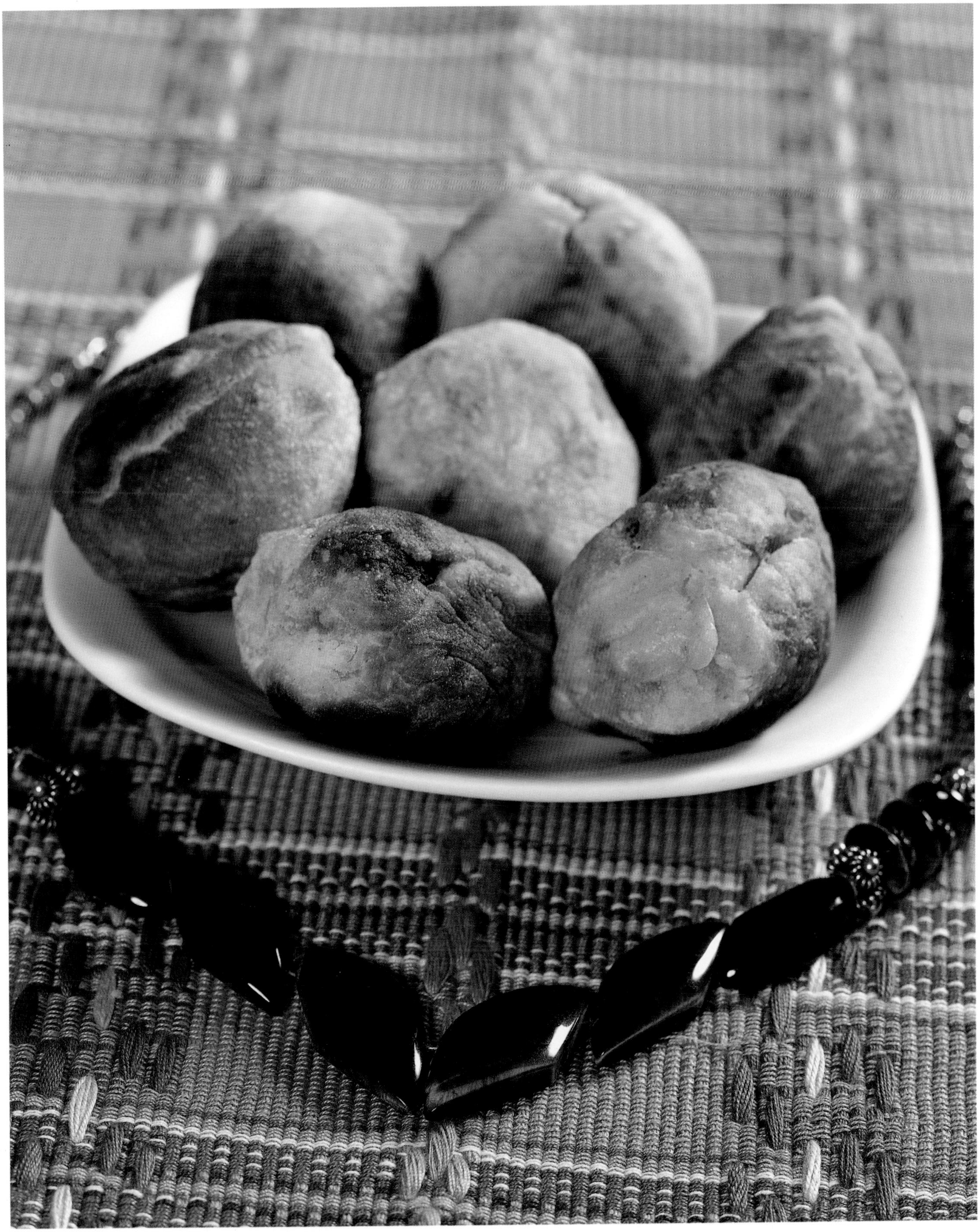

British

Fish & Chips 24
Toad in the Hole 26
Steak & Kidney Pie 28

Near the Silali Crater in the Rift Valley.
The beauty of Kenya at sunrise. A new day begins in this impressive valley between Lake Turkana and Nairobi. This area includes lush grasslands, barren deserts, and several soda lakes.

Missionaries at railway line, 1898

Kenya as a country developed from the European scramble for Africa, which was motivated by the urge for more territories, the demand for cheap labour and raw materials to support the industrial revolution in Europe and its strategic position in relation to India and the Far East. The scramble thus marked the beginning of colonization and the establishment of colonial rule in Kenya. Formal colonization, however, did not begin until the colonial powers set out the rules for claiming territories to lessen the possibility of war among themselves.

To the British, Kenya was strategic as it provided access to Uganda. Uganda in turn was of strategic importance because it was the source of the River Nile and therefore regarded as important for the control of Egypt and the Suez Canal. The forging of the colonial state began with a complete restructuring of indigenous institutions and ways of life.

The colonial administration appointed chiefs, who were given administrative, judicial and executive powers over the people in their area. After establishing Kenya as a protectorate in 1895, the British moved to consolidate colonial rule in Kenya in a number of phases. The Government began by building the Kenya-Uganda Railway as a means of quick communication between the coast and its Uganda and Sudan possessions. Later, the railway line was to tap the rich land lying inland from the coast to Uganda.

It also served as a basis for import-export trade. There were 60,000 white settlers living in Kenya in 1965. Today, there are an estimated 30,000 whites in Kenya. They formerly clustered in the country's highland region, the so-called "White Highlands", where the Cholmondeley (Delamere) family, as one of the few remaining white landowners, still owns over 100,000 acres (400 km²) of farmland in the Rift Valley. Nowadays, only a small minority of the British are still landowners (livestock and game ranchers, horticulturists and farmers), whereas the majority work in the tertiary sector: in finance, import, air transport, and hospitality.

Apart from isolated individuals such as anthropologist and conservationist Richard Leakey, who has retired, Kenyan white people have virtually completely retreated from Kenyan politics, and are no longer represented in public service and parastatals, from which the last remaining staff from colonial times retired in the 1970s.

BRITISH

Fish & Chips

Ingredients

250g plain flour
500ml milk or water
salt and freshly ground black pepper
900g potatoes
sunflower oil, for deep-frying
4 x 150g flat fish fillets - tilapia or red snapper

Method

Sift the flour into a large bowl and gradually whisk in the milk or water to give a smooth, thin batter (you may not need all of the liquid). Season, to taste, with salt and freshly ground black pepper. (this batter can be made up to eight hours in advance and kept in the fridge until needed.)
Peel the potatoes, if preferred, then cut into square-sided chips each about 1 inch thick. Wash and dry the chips well and set aside. Add the chips to the oil, a few handfuls at a time, and cook for 8-10 minutes or until soft but not browned. Remove with a slotted spoon, drain well and set aside. Heat the oil. At this point the chips can be cooled and placed in the fridge for up to 24 hours until needed.
Dip a fish fillet in the batter to coat evenly, then carefully lower into the hot oil. Deep-fry for 3-4 minutes, or until crisp, golden-brown and cooked through, turning halfway through cooking. Remove and drain well on kitchen paper, keep warm. To finish the chips, deep-fry them in batches until crisp and golden-brown. Drain on kitchen paper and season lightly with salt and freshly ground black pepper. Serve with the chips, vinegar and a small bowl of tartare sauce for sharing.

Serves 3.

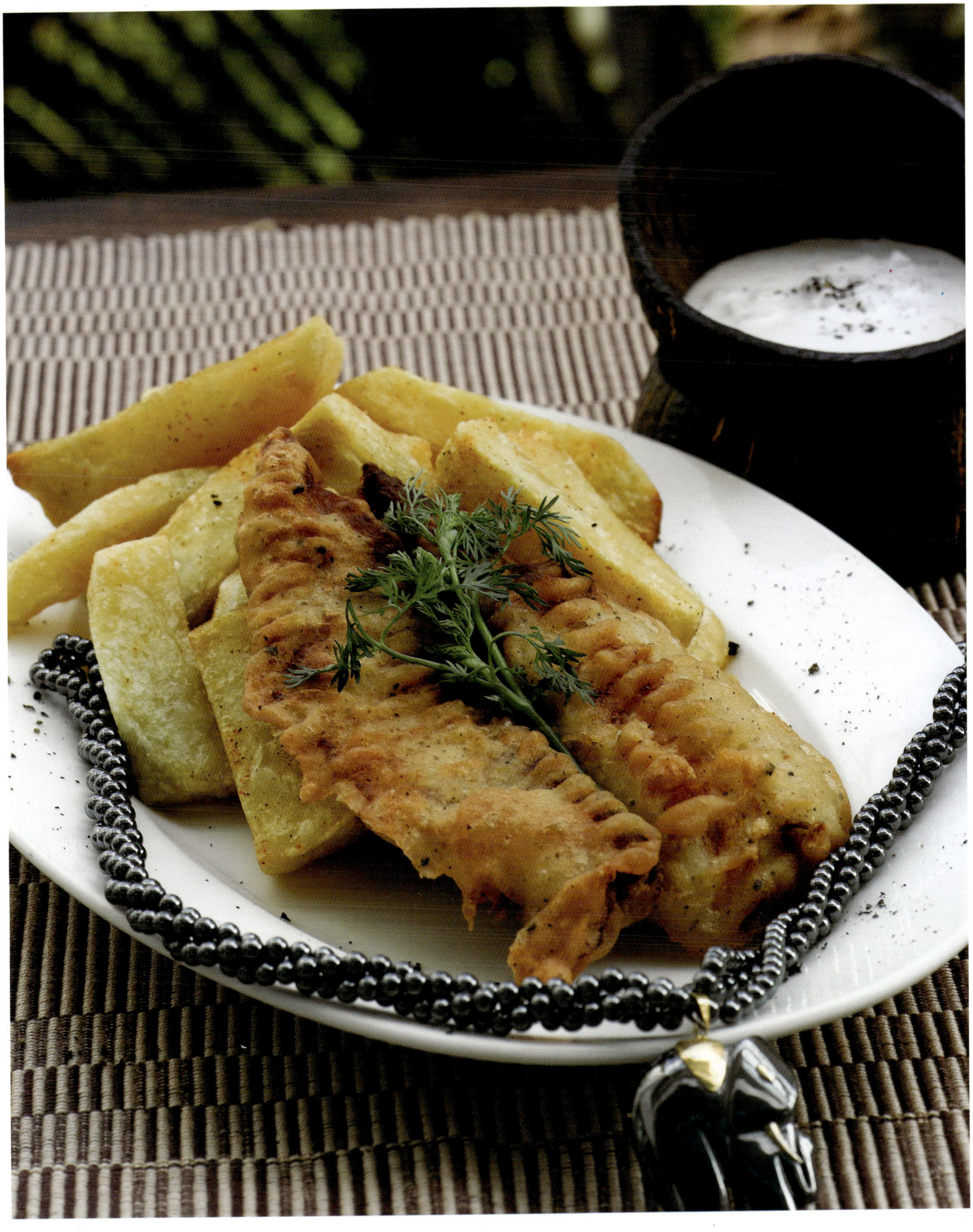

Toad in The Hole

BRITISH

Ingredients

115g plain flour
large pinch of salt
freshly ground black pepper
4 large free-range eggs
300ml pint milk
2 tbsp fresh thyme leaves
8 good quality pork or beef sausages
1 tbsp mustard powder
2 tbsp of white vegetable fat
knob of butter, to serve

Method

To make the batter, sift the flour into a large bowl. Add the salt and pepper. Make a hole in the centre of the flour and crack in the eggs. Gradually beat the eggs into the flour then slowly beat in the milk. Strain and push any remaining lumps through a sieve. Stir in the thyme. Cover and leave to stand for 30 minutes, or ideally 3-4 hours. Preheat the oven to 200C.
Heat a large non-stick pan and cook the sausages over a medium heat until golden-brown all over. (If you do not have a non-stick pan add a little oil.) Turn off the heat and brush the sausages with the mustard. Set aside.
Place the vegetable fat into an ovenproof dish and heat in the oven for five minutes or until it is hot and hazy. Add the sausages to the hot dish and pour in the batter. Immediately return the dish to the oven and cook for 35-40 minutes until well-risen and golden-brown.
Serve seasoned with black pepper and a large knob of butter.

Serves 3.

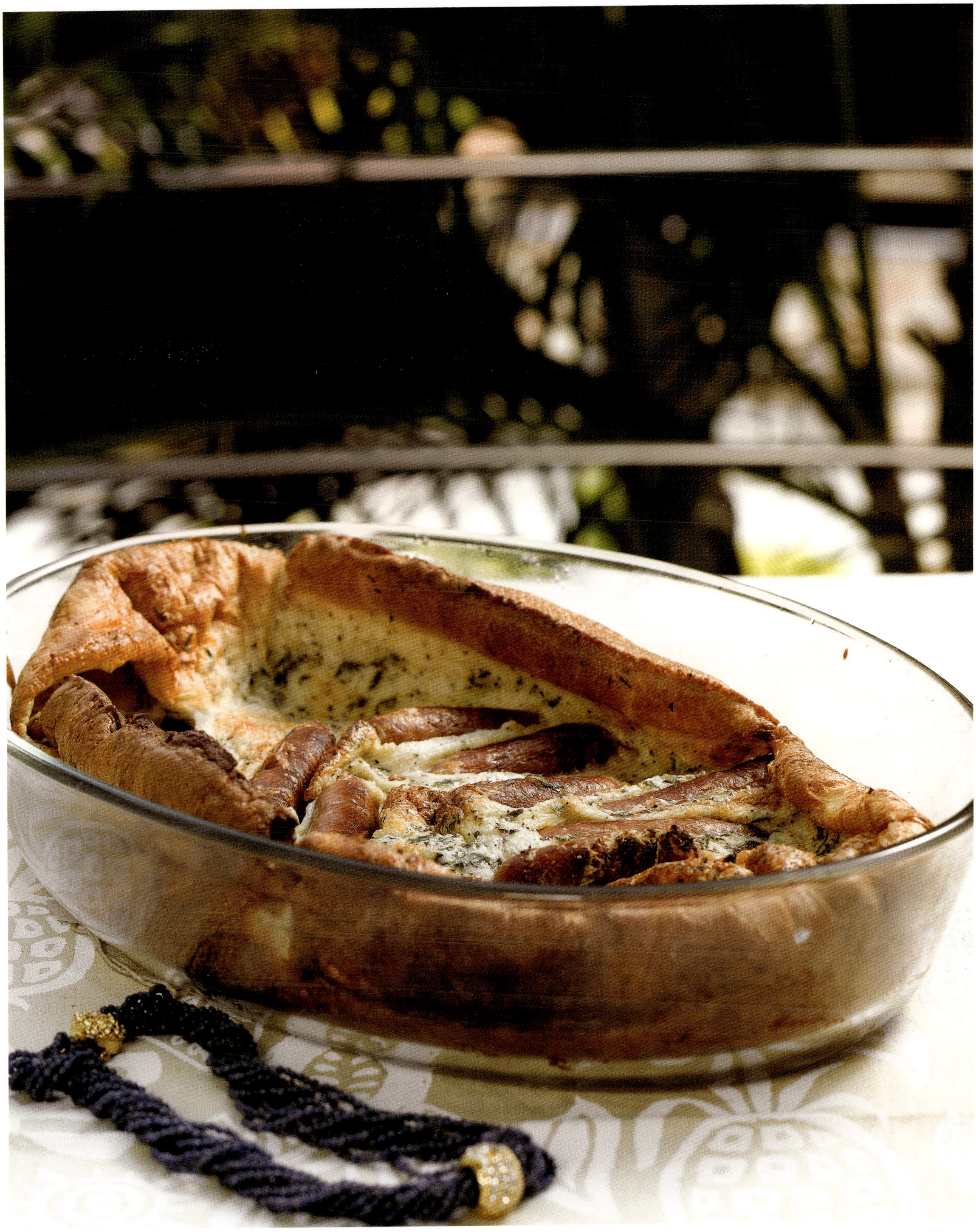

BRITISH

Steak & Kidney Pie

Ingredients

for the base
300g puff pastry
1 egg and 1 extra egg yolk beaten together
for the filling
2 tbsp vegetable oil
700g stewing beef, diced
200g lamb or ox kidney, diced
2 medium onions, diced

30g plain flour
850ml pints beef stock
salt and freshly ground black pepper, to taste
a dash of worcestershire sauce

Method

Heat the vegetable oil in a large frying pan, and use to seal the beef. Remove and set to one side.
Brown the kidney in the same pan. Add the onions and cook for 3-4 minutes.
Return the meat to the pan, sprinkle flour over and coat the meat and onions.
Add the stock to the pan, stir well and bring to the boil.
Turn the heat down and simmer for 1½ hours without a lid. If the liquid evaporates too much, add more stock.
Remove from the heat. Add salt, pepper and Worcestershire sauce and allow to cool slightly.
Place the cooked meat mixture into a pie dish.
Roll out the pastry to ¼in thick and 2in larger than the dish you are using.
Using a rolling pin, lift the pastry and place it over the top of the pie dish.
Trim and crimp the edges with your fingers and thumb.
Brush the surface with the beaten egg mixture. Bake for 30-40 minutes at 220C.
Serve with peas and carrots.

Serves 3.

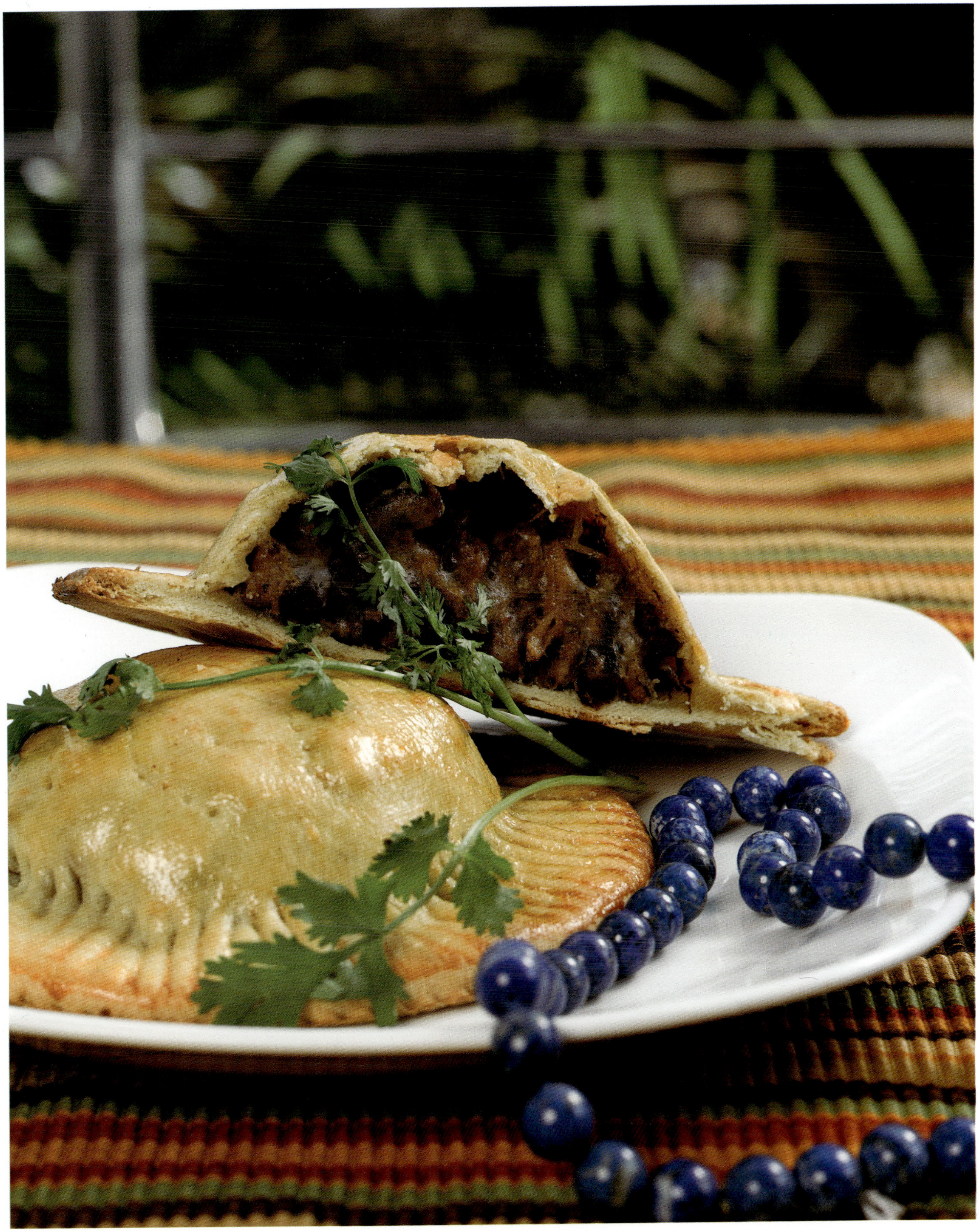

30

Indian

Masala Chicken   34
Chili Paneer Pasanda   36
Black Lentil Curry   38

Lake Nakuru.
Lesser flamingos as far as the eye can see. This shallow saline lake in the Rift Valley is world famous for its huge numbers of flamingos. At times, the lake hosts up to two million of these pink-plumaged birds at once. However, it is the nutrition available in the lake at any given time that determines the number of birds.

Indians at Bishops house, Kisauni, 1896.

Indians in Kenya generally refers to people from the South Asian subcontinent: from India, Pakistan, Bangladesh and Sri Lanka. The Indian community largely comes from the 32,000 indentured laborers brought in to build the cross-country railroad from Kenya to Uganda in the late 1800s.

When their contracts expired, many of these people settled down in Kenya. It's interesting to note that about 2,500 workers died during the construction of the railway - four for each mile of track laid. Much of the track ran through the inhospitable territory of what is now the Tsavo Game Park, and more than 140 of the workers were killed by man-eating lions. This was a high price to pay.

Over the years, Indians have made tremendous contribution to Kenya's economy and culture. Preferential treatment given to Europeans after independence confined Indians mainly to a middlemen role that prevented them from participating fully in the development of Kenya. However, Indians economic activity has been flourishing again since market liberalization policies gathered momentum in the 1990s.

Nakuru is populated by people from the whole of Kenya and from many regions of the world. The town has a sizeable population of Kenyans of Indian origin and a few of the original settler families also remained in the area.

INDIAN

Masala Chicken

Ingredients

1 whole chicken or 1 kg chicken breasts cut
1 tsp cumin seeds
½ cup oil
3 big onions, chopped
3 cloves of garlic, crushed
1 inch piece ginger, crushed
2-3 green chillies, chopped
handful fenugreek leaves

1 tbsp coriander powder
4 tomatoes, chopped
1 tsp tomato paste
1 tbsp garam masala
salt and red chilli powder to taste
½ tbsp turmeric powder
corriander leaves (dania)

Method

Clean and cut the chicken into pieces.
Heat oil and fry the onions until golden with cumin seeds.
Add coriander powder, fenugreek leaves and stir.
Add ground green chillies, garlic, ginger, salt, turmeric and chilli powder, cooking till oil is seen over the onions.
Add tomatoes and tomato paste and cook a few minutes more. Add the chicken and mix.
Add water if you need the chicken with a curry gravy.
Cook chicken on medium heat covered, stirring until it is ready.
Finally add garam masala and coriander leaves.
To make it creamy you can add 2 tbsp of fresh cream.

Serves 5.

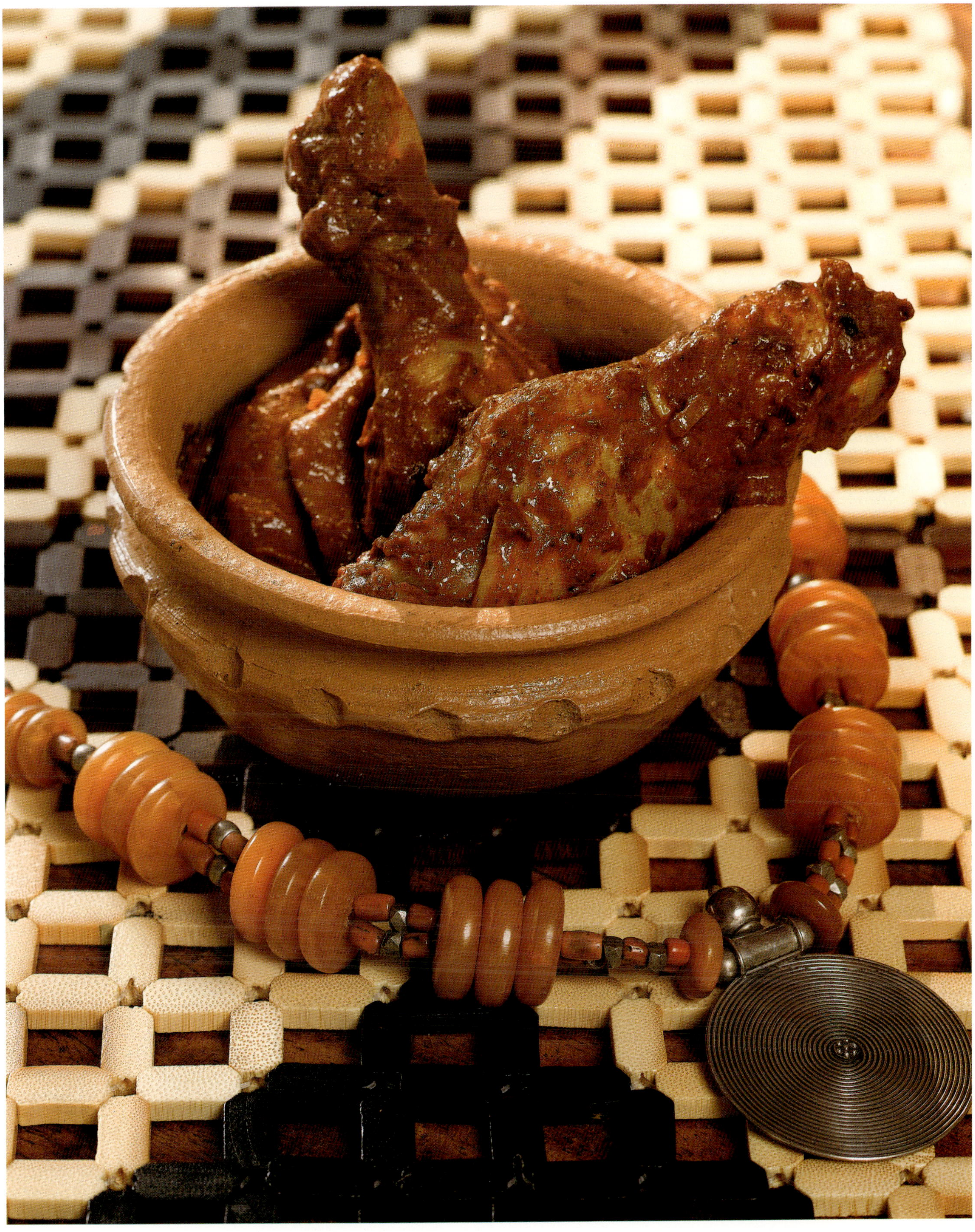

INDIAN

Chili Paneer Pasanda

Ingredients

250g paneer cut into long strips
2 onions, sliced
1 capsicum, sliced
2 tomatoes, grated
2 tsp tomato paste
2 tsp coriander powder
3 green chillies, chopped
1 tsp garam masala

4 garlic cloves, crushed
½ inch piece ginger, crushed
1 tsp cumin powder, roasted
½ tsp ajwain powder (celery or tymol seeds)
8 tbsp oil
2 tbsp butter
2 tbsp coriander, chopped

Method

Deep fry paneer until it is golden and keep it aside.
Sauté the onions until golden.
Adding the butter, tomatoes, chillies, garlic, ginger, tomato paste, fry for 2 to 3 minutes.
Add all the dry spices except cumin and ajwain.
Add paneer and capsicum and stir fry for 5 minutes.
Add cumin and ajwain powder and mix well.
Sprinkle with fresh coriander.

Serves 2.

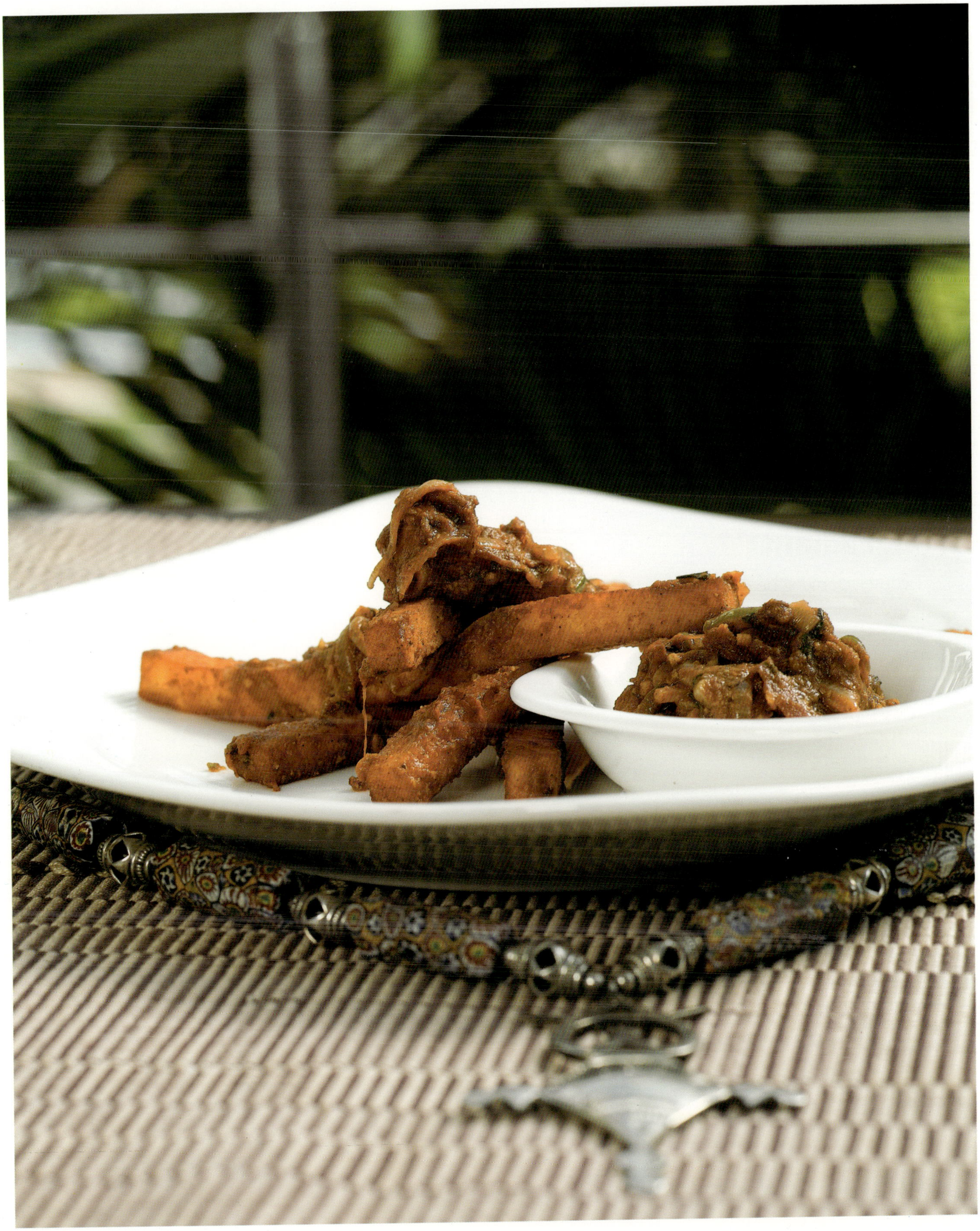

INDIAN

Black Lentil Curry

Ingredients

1 cup black mung beans (ndengu)
2 onions, finely chopped
3 tomatoes, chopped
½ tsp turmeric powder
¾ green chilli (slit in centre)
½ inch piece ginger, crushed

1 tsp cumin seeds
salt and chilli powder
100g butter
2 tbsp ghee
handful coriander leaves

Method

Soak black lentils in 4 cups of water overnight.
Heat ghee in a pressure cooker pot and put in onions and ginger and cook until golden brown, add cumin seeds.
Add tomatoes, salt, chilli powder and turmeric powder and cook. Keep cooking until the ghee leaves the sides. Add lentils and 2 cups of water and pressure cook until 7/8 whistles.
Open when cool and check if lentils are soft and tender. Continue to cook until well done and runny. Add green chilli, coriander leaves and butter.

Serves 3.

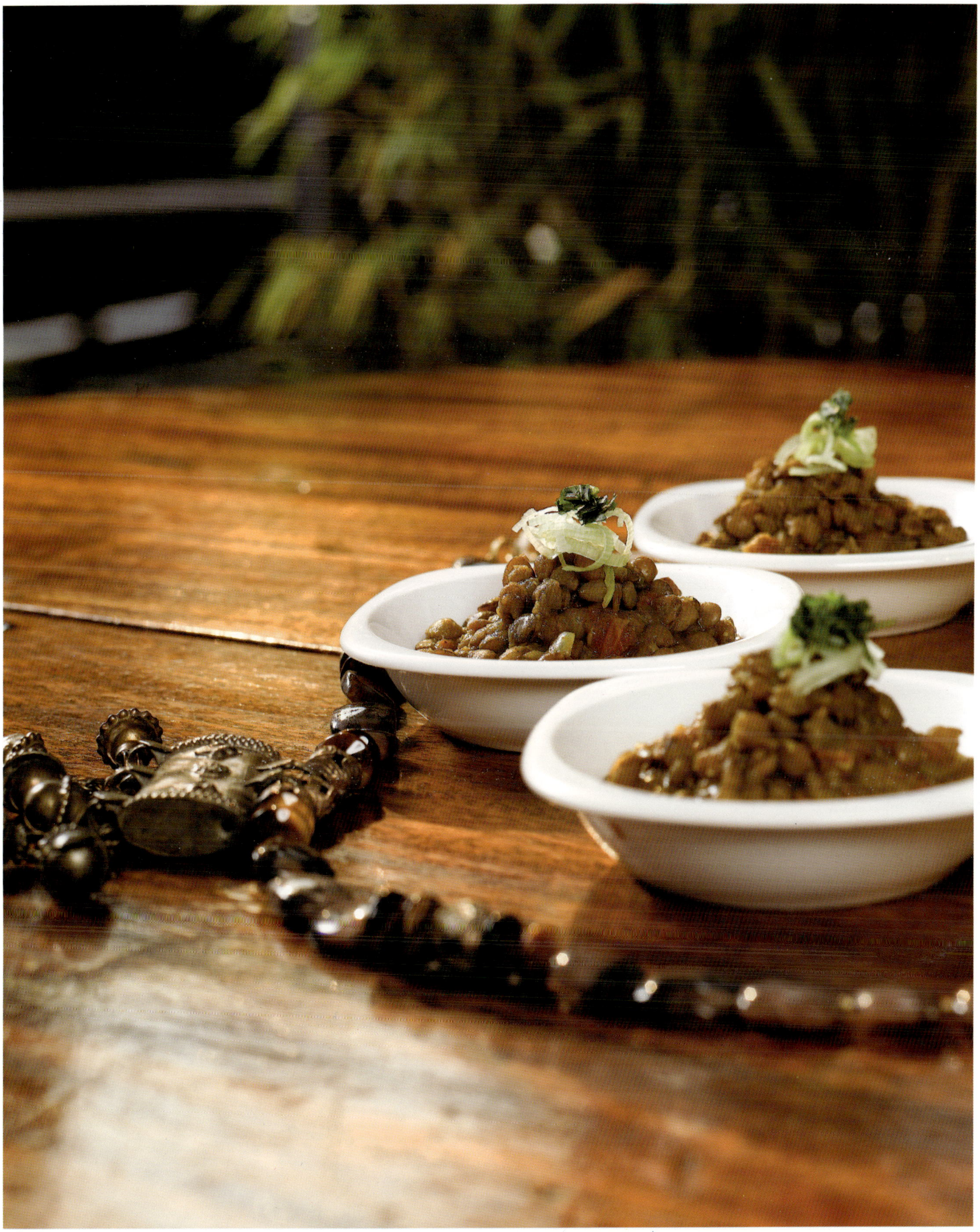

Kalenjin

Mushebebit 44
Boinnet 46
Magrek 48

East of the Suguta Valley.
It rains more on the graben shoulder than in the valley, which is why it's greener here than in many other portions of the Sugutu Valley. The valley sank as the earth's crust expanded, allowing rivers to cut through and form this landscape.

Kipsigis married woman

The Kalenjin community belongs to a Nilotic ethnic group. These highland Nilotes include eight culturally and linguistically related groups, namely Kipsigis, Nandi, Tugen, Marakwet, Keiyo, Pokot, Sabaot, Ongiek and Terik.

The Kalenjin are renowned on a national and international level for their athletic prowess and they are sometimes referred to as Kenya's running tribe. They are traditionally pastoralists and occupy the fertile Rift Valley Province.

The Kalenjin hold their cattle in very high regard and most of them are still engaged both in farming and animal husbandry. Traditionally they built round homes made of sticks and mud plaster, usually with pointed thatch roofs with a pole out the centre. The children of Kalenjin were taught to respect elders. Girls were taught to kneel before men and were not supposed to speak to men until they had gone through circumcision. Boys were not allowed to sleep in the same house with their mother after the age of 5 years.

Customary Kalenjin clothing was made of the skins of either domesticated or wild animals. Both male and female Kalenjin wore earrings made of heavy brass coils that stretched the ear lobe down to shoulder level. Even though the Kalenjin are not very well known for their handicrafts, women make and sell beautifully decorated calabashes. They are rubbed with oil and adorned with small coloured beads.

The Sabaot people live on Mount Elgon, an extinct volcano crisscrossed by mountain streams and spectacular waterfalls. The Kenya-Uganda border goes straight through the mountain-top, cutting the Sabaot homeland into two halves.

KALENJIN

Mushebebit

Ingredients

10 cups pumpkin leaves, shredded
½ cup fresh milk
2 tbsp munyet

Method

Shred the leaves with your bare hands and then boil them in 'munyet' for five minutes.
How to make 'munyet': Use dried bean pods and burn them.
Collect this ash and then put it in a container that has holes.
Fill the container with water and then collect the liquid that comes through the holes.
That is munyet and you only need to use two spoons per dish.
Once you have boiled the vegetables for 5 minutes, add fresh milk.

Serves 3.

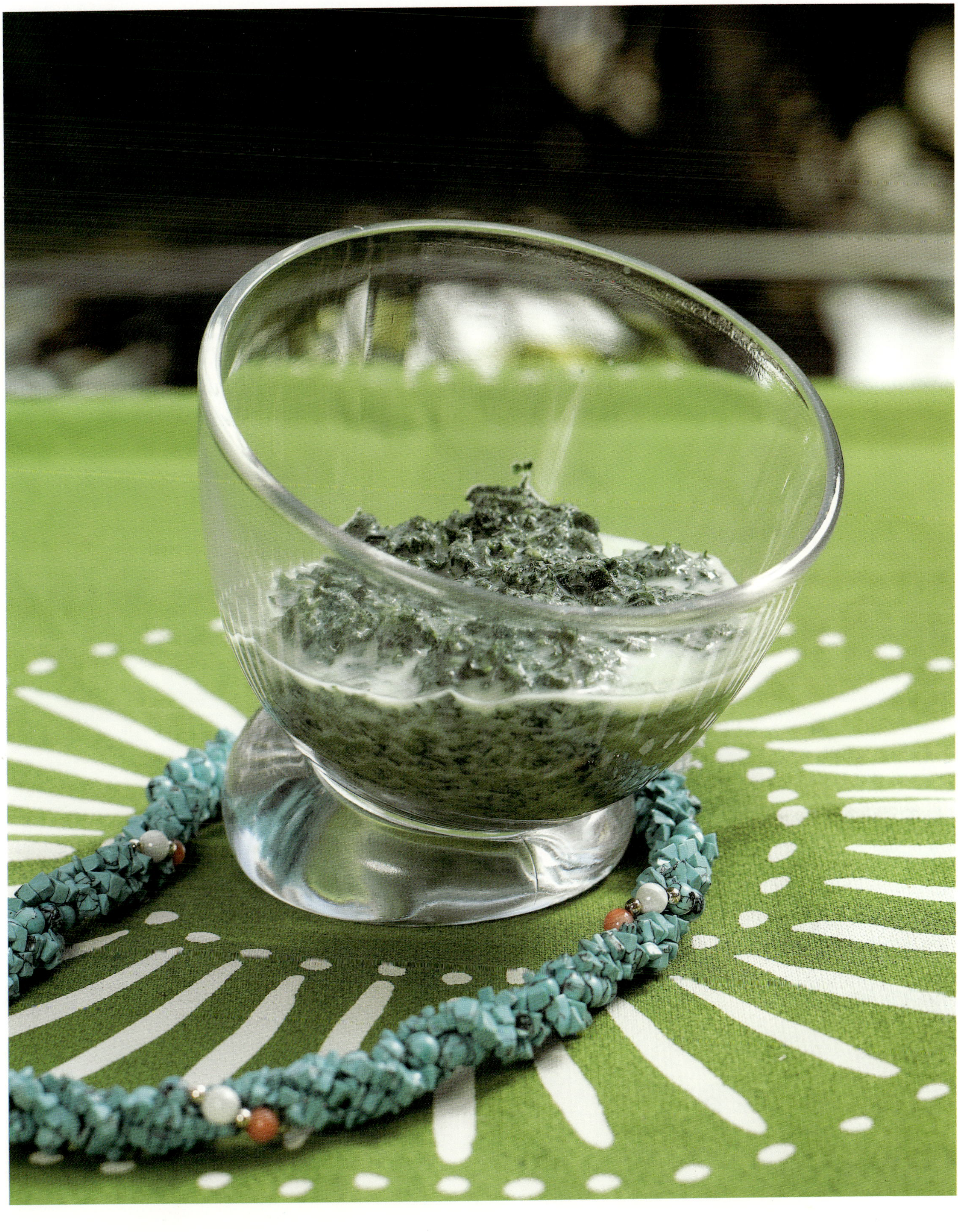

KALENJIN

Boinnet

Ingredients

1 kg fresh game meat (dik dik, antelope, buffalo)

Method

Cut the raw meat into strips.
Roast the meat over an open fire on skewers.

The Ongiek had huge drums for storing honey in their huts and used these to preserve meat. The strips of meat were then totally submerged in honey and could be preserved in that state for up to 2 years. They also drank the animal blood which was only allowed from a herbivore. Honey was a valuable commodity in every home.

Serves 3.

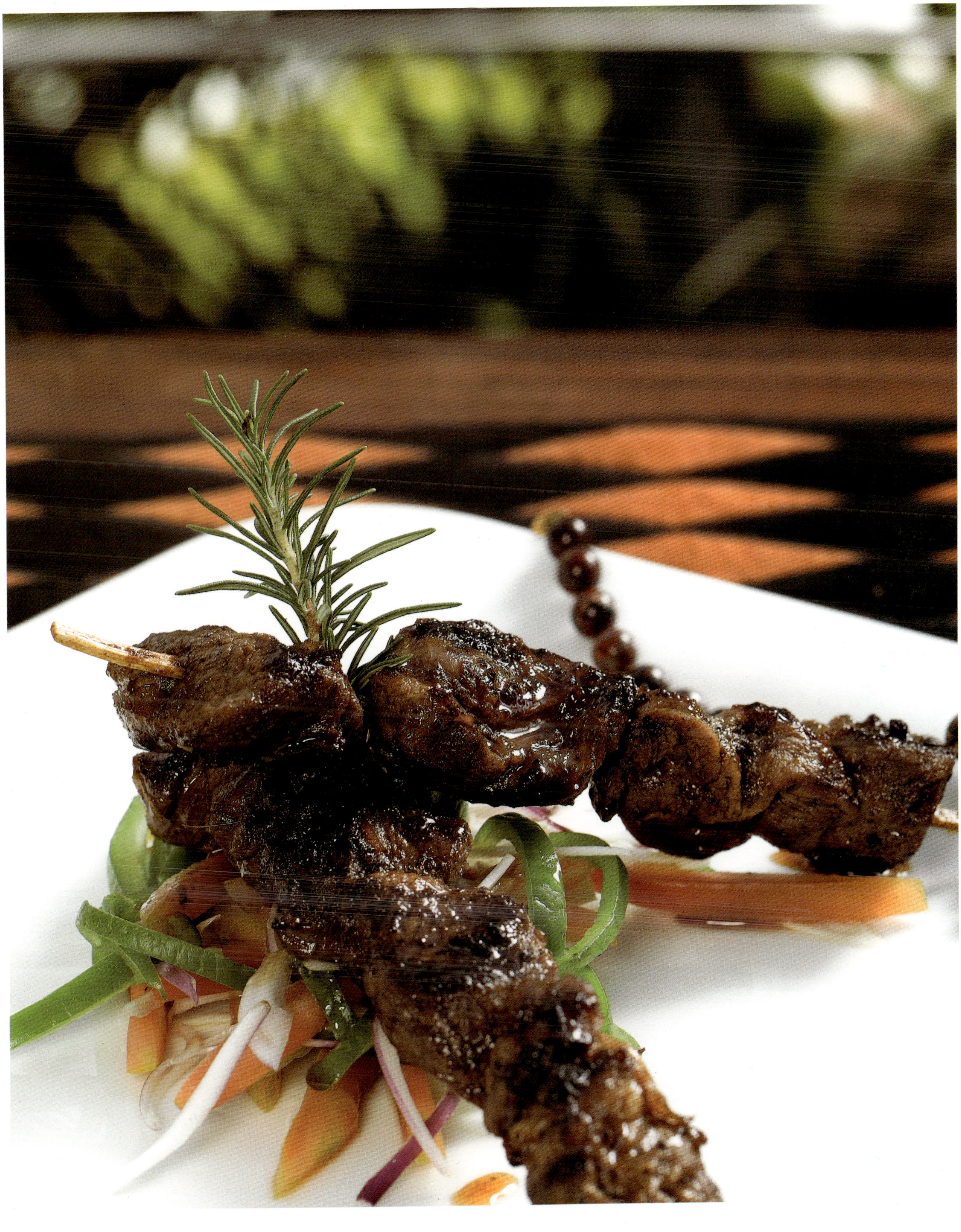

KALENJIN

Magrek

Ingredients
3 cups rose coco beans
2 cups fresh milk

Method
Roast the beans and then use a stone to pound them until you remove the top skin.
Ensure that all the husks are blown off and then boil the beans in munyet so that they become soft.
Mash them into a paste and then add fresh milk.

Serves 3.

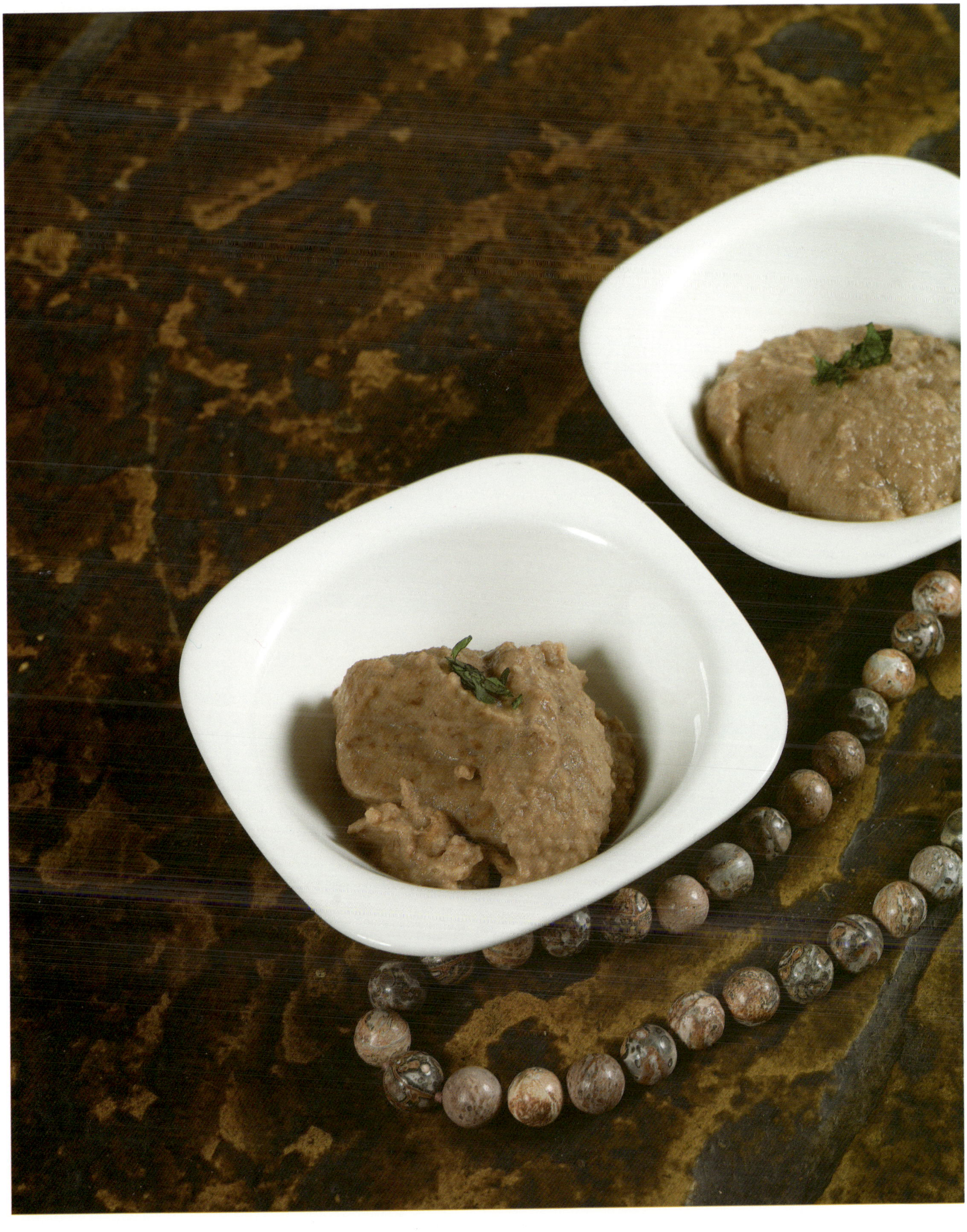

50

Kamba

Ngunza Kutu   54
Kinaa   56
Muthokoi   58

Chyulu Hills.
A landscape shortly before sunset. This volcanic mountain range is near Tsavo West National Park. Along with the impressive mountain forest, there are riverside forests, forested grasslands, hot springs, and large open plains.

Kamba young woman

The Kamba are a Bantu ethnic group who live in the semi-arid Eastern Province of Kenya and as a result were traders in cane beer, ivory, brass amulets, tools and weapons, millet and cattle. The food obtained from trading helped offset shortages caused by droughts and famines. The Kamba are still known for their fine work in basketry and pottery. Their artistic inclination is evidenced in the sculpture work that is on display in many craft shops.

They served as intermediaries between the coast and up country – acting as guides to Swahili and Arab caravans, the Kamba were naturally enlisted by early European arrivals in East Africa as guides and porters. According to their oral history, the Kamba were originally semi nomadic and possessed large herds of cattle, like the neighboring Maasai. Unlike the Maasai however, they did not rely exclusively on cattle but also practiced cultivation, gathered edible plants and roots and hunted using traps.

As the colonization of Kenya continued, the Kamba did not lose as much of their land as some other communities did due to its dry and somewhat unproductive climate. Though they did not lose as much land as others, they did lose their unique trade routes with the coming of the British railway through the country.

The Kamba economy was to later suffer huge set-backs occasioned by the loss of cattle to rinderpest, the arrival of the Europeans, and the subsequent ban on further expansion. With their land no longer fertile, natural erosion setting in and their unwillingness to cut down on their herds, the land finally gave in and triggered long spells of drought and famine, infamous to this day.

KAMBA

Ngunza Kutu

Ingredients
5 handfuls cow pea leaves (kunde)
1 onion, chopped
salt to taste
4tbsp ghee
5 cups maize meal flour

Method
Boil the leaves of cow peas for a short time then put in salt and onion. Add some maize flour into this mixture and stir it into a semi firm mixture. Add the ghee.

This was eaten during famine.

Serves 5.

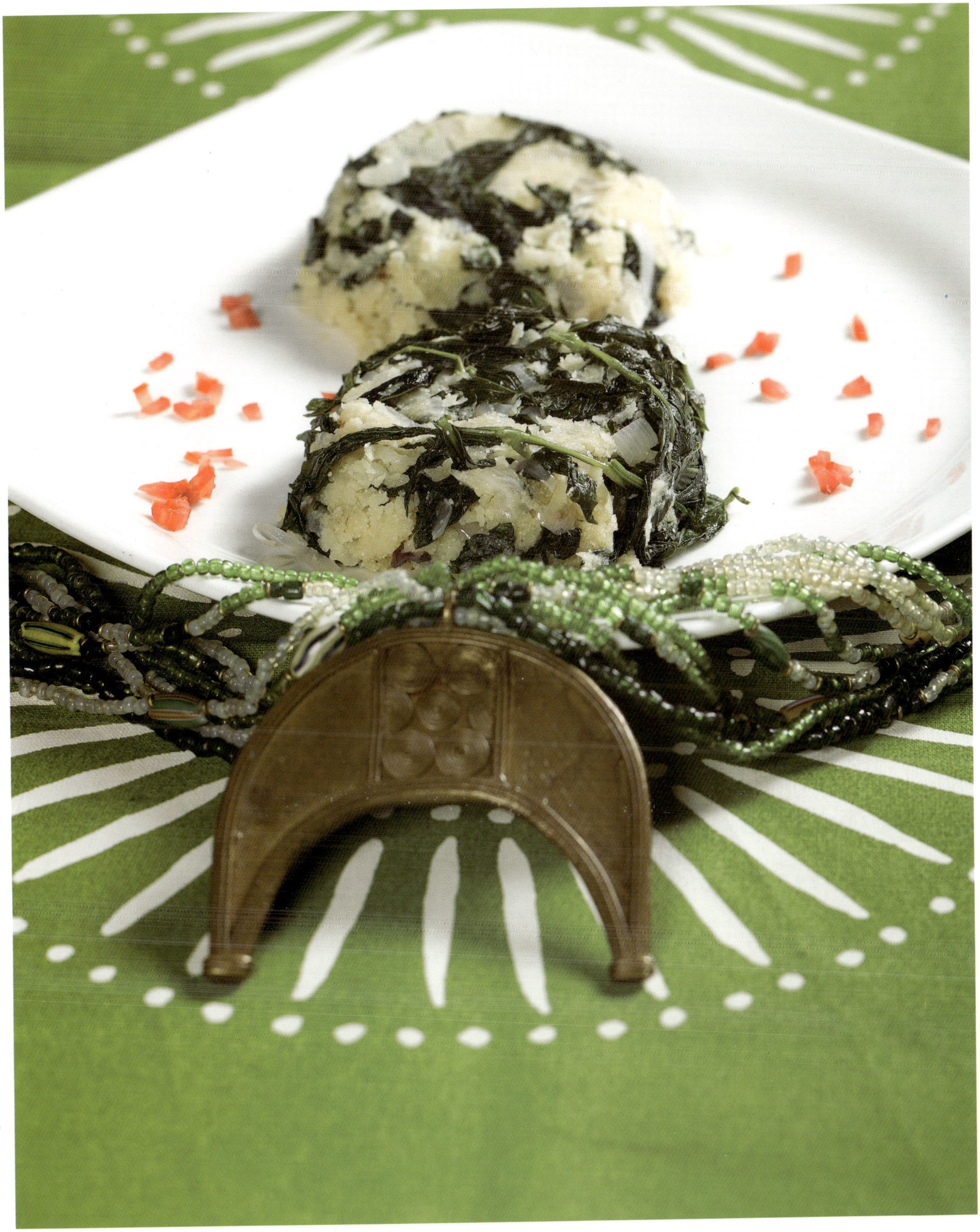

KAMBA

Kinaa

Ingredients

2 cups mwee (finger millet)
maziwa lala (fermented milk) to your desired consistency

Method

Finely grind mwee with the traditional stone.
Then add mala (fermented milk) according to your desired consistency.
You can make it thick like ugali or thin like porridge.

School going children used to carry it for lunch or when herding animals.

Serves 3.

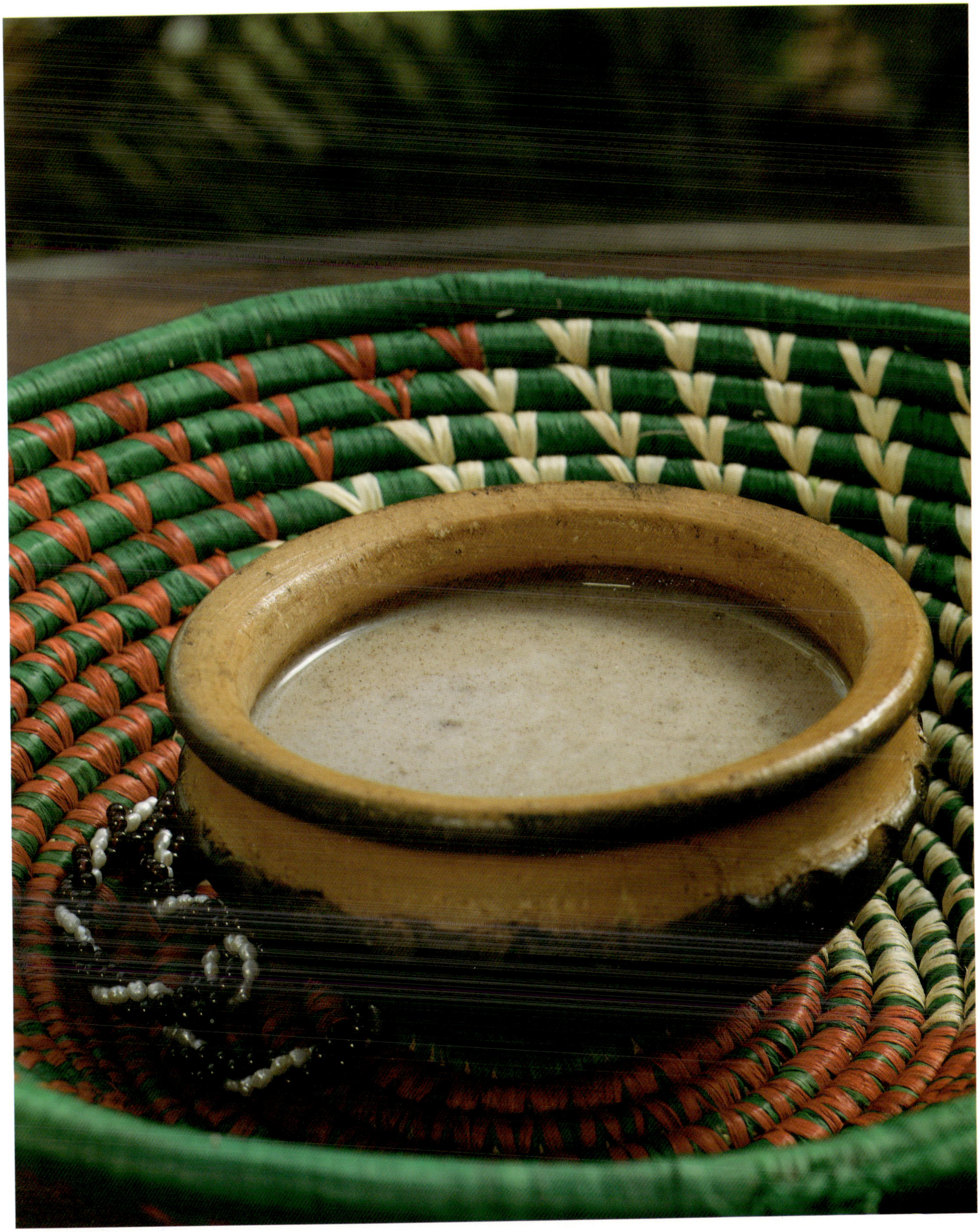

KAMBA

Muthokoi

Ingredients

4 cups dry maize kernels, pounded (muthokoi)
1 large whole piece cassava
3 cups pigeon peas (mbaazi)
1 onion, chopped
3 tbsp ghee
salt to taste

Method

Individually pre-boil the cassava, pigeon peas (one can also use red beans or cow peas) and the maize.
Make sure you remove the string from the centre of the cassava.
Fry onion with oil until just turning golden brown.
Add the cassava, pigeon peas and maize and mash.
Add salt and serve.

Serves 5.

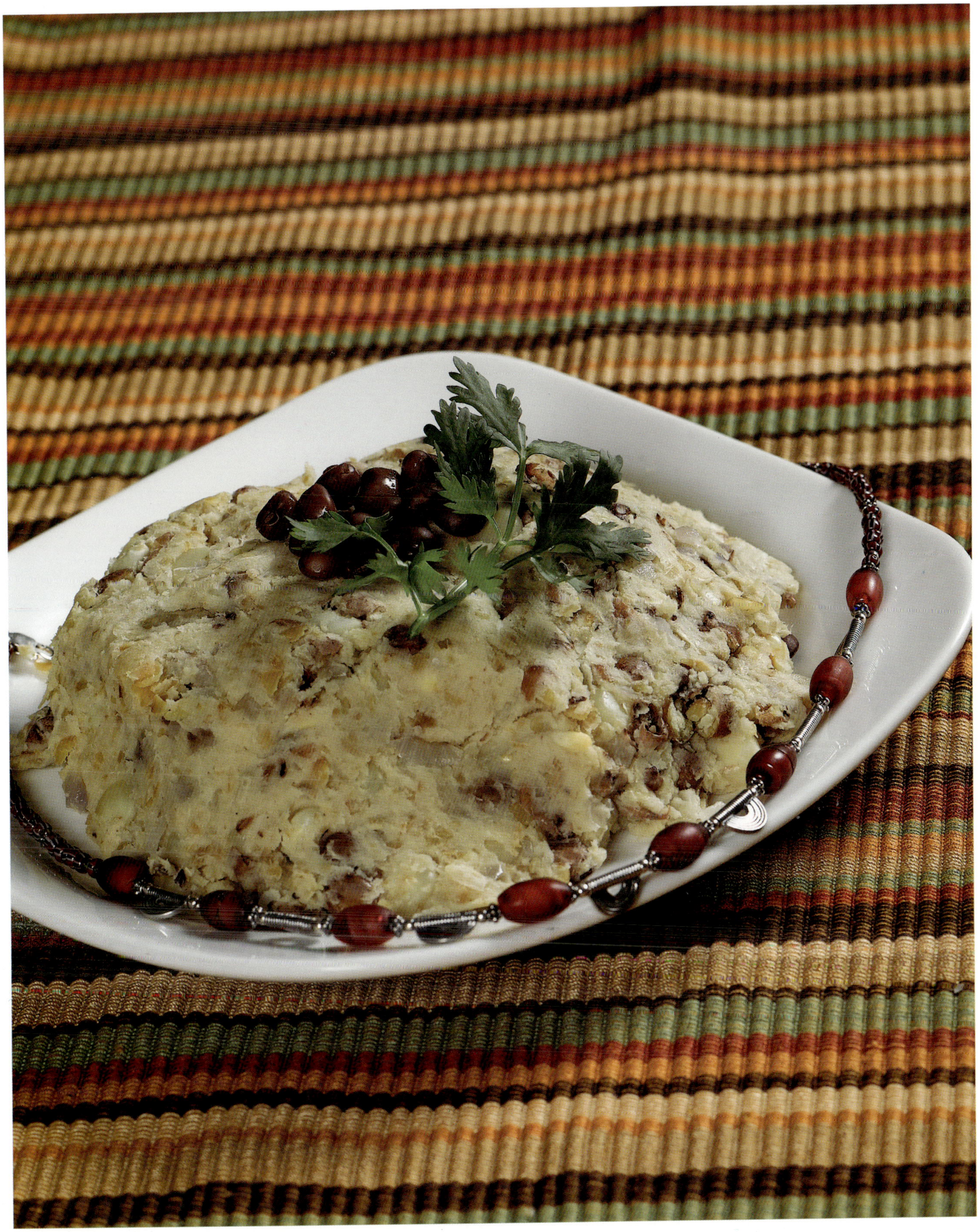

60

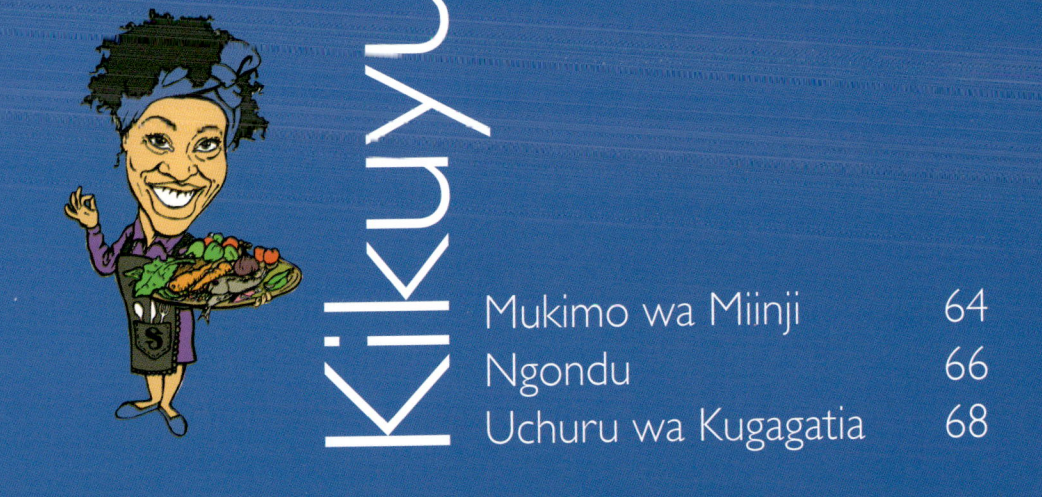

Kikuyu

Mukimo wa Miinji	64
Ngondu	66
Uchuru wa Kugagatia	68

Aberdare National Park, Karuru Falls.
This park offers a fascinating variety of landscapes, mountain peaks, valleys, streams, rivers, but also moors, stands of bamboo and rainforest at lower elevations. You can also see impressive waterfalls like Karuru Falls, where the water thunders down 920 ft. over three separate drops.

Kikuyu Elder in ngoma dress

While the Kikuyu can be found throughout Kenya and indeed the world, the heaviest concentration is in Central Province. The Kikuyu's contact with the outside world came through missionaries and settlers. The name for the mountain around which they settled, Mt. Kenya is actually a Kamba word because it was a Kamba guide who led the first white person there.

Their proximity to the British colonial government in Nairobi and the settlers who desired the comfortable central highlands simultaneously gave them a great advantage and imposed on them the greatest burden of peoples under colonialism. Many of them developed a greater adaptability and used the British colonial system to overcome the system.

The Kikuyu are traditionally an industrious agricultural people who are very proud of their language and most multilingual Kikuyu prefer to speak Kikuyu with anyone who knows the language. Music and dance are strong components of the Kikuyu culture, with a vigorous recording industry.

Kikuyu's traditional belief was that whistling was a taboo, it would call malicious spirits. They also believed that the number 10 was unlucky and when counting they used to say "full nine" instead of the word for ten.

The Mau Mau were a militant African nationalist movement active in Kenya in the 1950s whose main aim was to remove British rule and European settlers from the country. Members, who were mostly made up of Kikuyus, were required to take an oath to drive the white man from Kenya. In November 1952, Jomo Kenyatta was arrested and charged with managing the Mau Mau terrorist society in Kenya and sentenced to seven years hard labor in Kapenguria. After imprisoning more than 70,000 Kikuyu tribesmen suspected of Mau Mau membership in 1955 a general amnesty is announced for Mau Mau activists in 1963.

KIKUYU

Mukimo wa Miinji

Ingredients

3 cups green maize kernals
3 cups green peas
6 cups kahurura, chopped (pumpkin leaves)
1 1/2kg potatoes, quartered
salt to taste

Method

Boil green maize and green peas until almost cooked and then add potatoes.
When these are almost cooked add the greens.
Put just enough water so that when the food is cooked there is no more water.
Mash together all ingredients thoroughly as you add salt to taste.

You can blanch the greens beforehand and blend them, and put them in the fridge.

Serves 5.

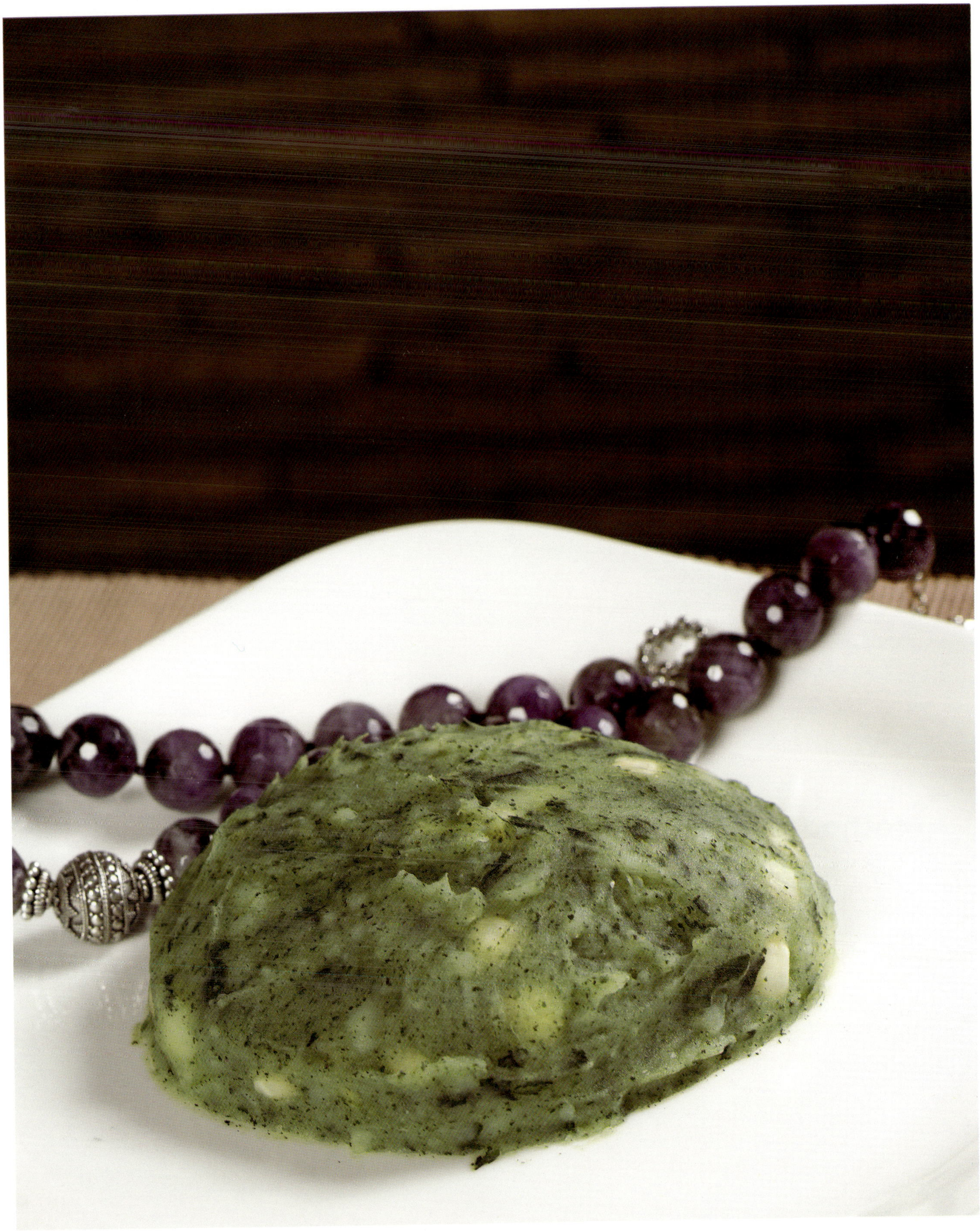

KIKUYU

Ngondu

Ingredients

½ cup spring onions, chopped
6 cloves of garlic, crushed
salt to taste
3 tomatoes, chopped
1kg lamb

Method

Cut the meat into medium size cubes and put into the pot.
Put in spring onions and garlic.
Add tomatoes into the pot.
Let this simmer in its own liquid and fat until cooked.
Then add salt and serve.

Serves 3.

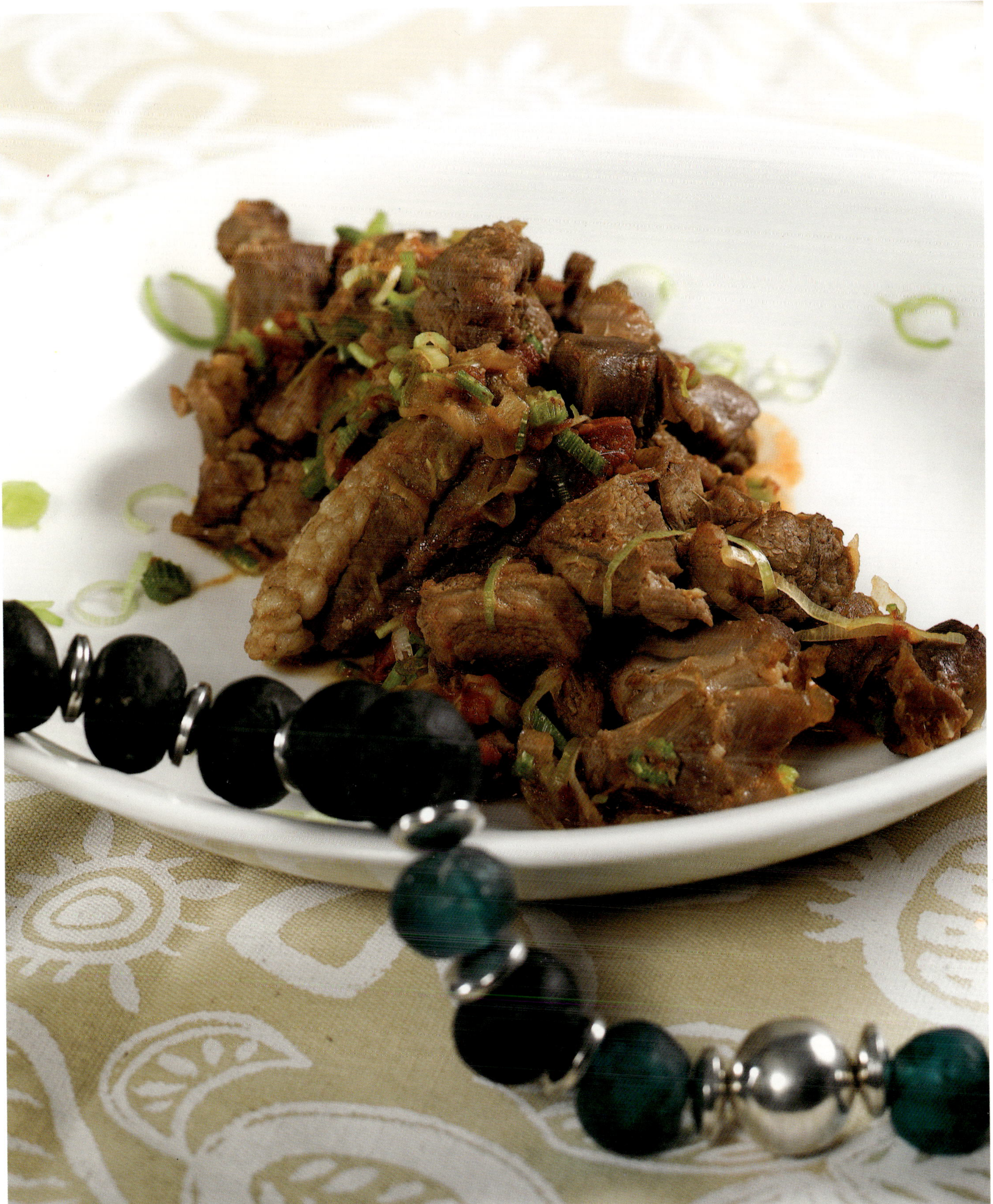

KIKUYU

Ucuru wa Kugagatia

Ingredients

2 cups dry maize kernals
2 cups dried millet grains
water to submerge
sugar to taste

Method

Use the traditional stone to grind the maize and the millet into the required consistency.
Ferment this flour mixture in water and then cook it into a runny porridge.
You can now buy the fermented mixture 'Kaheho'.
Add sugar if desired.

Serves 4.

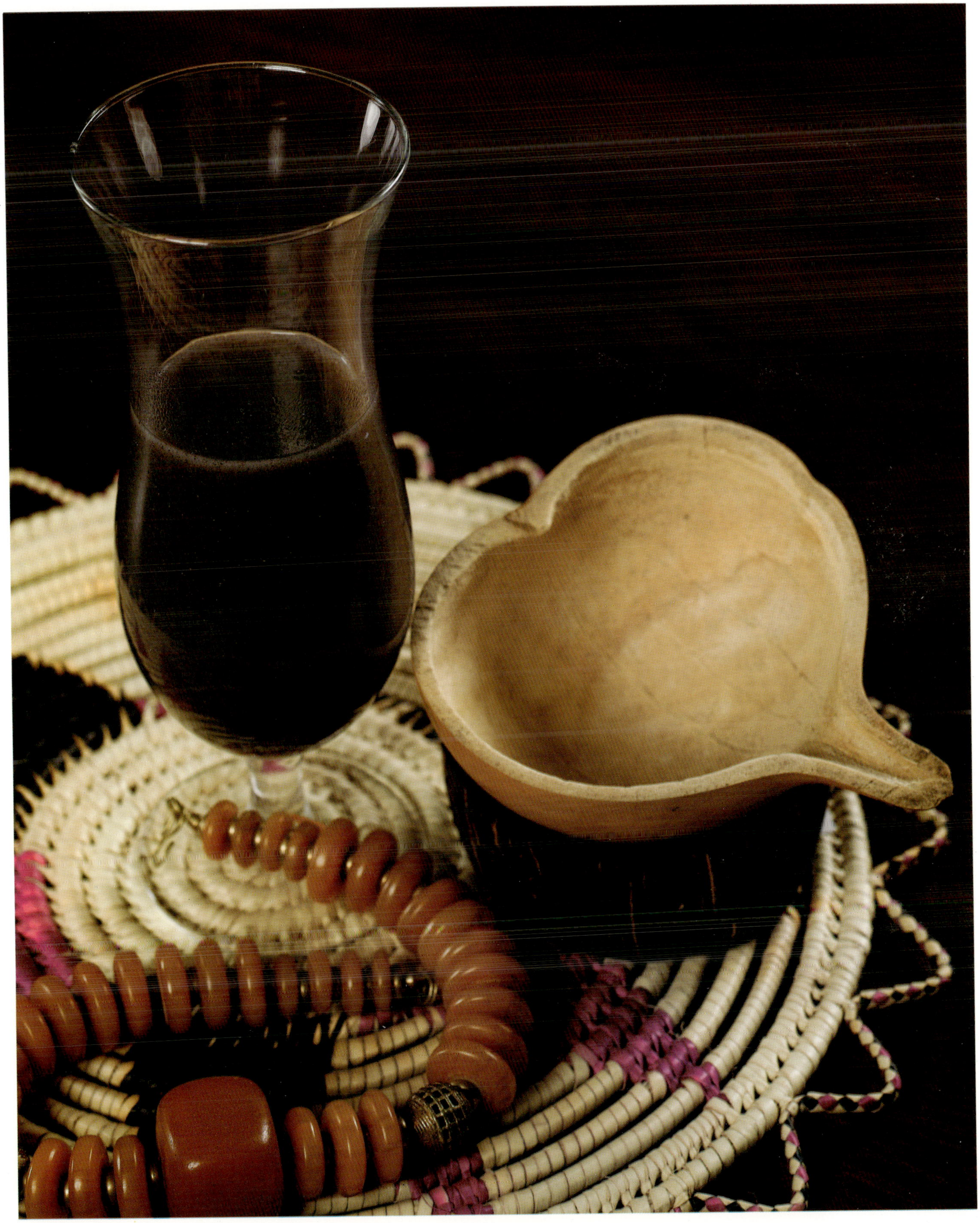

70

Kisii

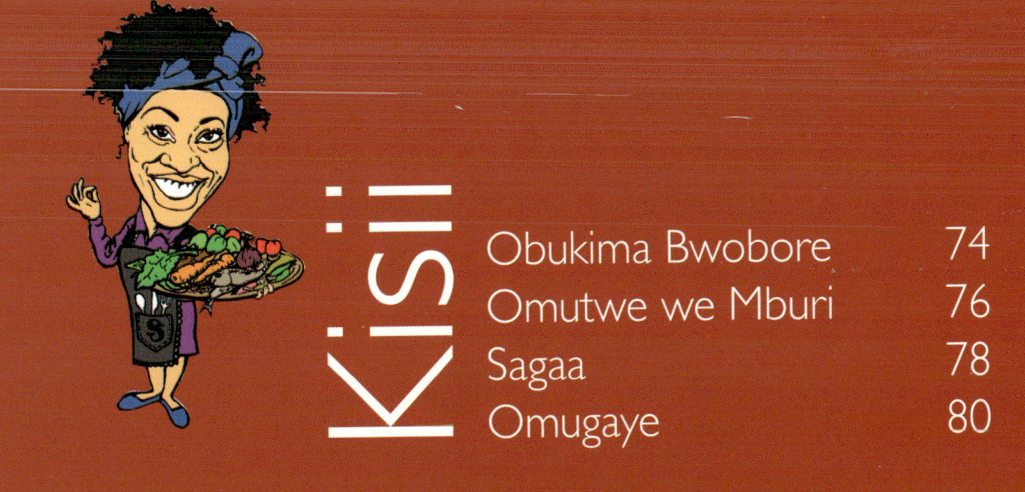

Obukima Bwobore	74
Omutwe we Mburi	76
Sagaa	78
Omugaye	80

Tea plantation, Nandi Hills.
The climate in the highlands, with evenly distributed rainfall and slightly acidic soil that holds water well, is optimal for growing tea leaves. Kenya is now one of the world's leading tea producers, just behind China and India. The primary customer for CTC tea is England, where strong, fresh tea is especially prized.

Kisii bridegroom

The Kisii are regarded as one of the most economically active communities in Kenya, with rolling tea estates, coffee, and banana groves as Kisii land is very fertile and often wet throughout the year. However, Kisii country has a very high population density. It is one of the most densely populated areas in Kenya (after the two cities of Nairobi and Mombasa), and the most densely populated rural area. It also has one of the highest fertility and population growth rates in Kenya (as evidenced by successive census and demographic surveys).

In fact the fertility rate of Kisii ranks among the highest in the world, (see Kenyan Conundrum: A Regional Analysis of Population Growth and Primary Education (Paperback) by Juha I. Uitto). These factors have ensured the Kisii to be among the most geographically widespread communities in East Africa.

Their closest ethnic group among the Bantu is the Meru, who have a similar language and culture. Kisii was one of the few Kenyan groups that practiced mandatory female circumcision, a ritual which has since been outlawed.

Driving through Kisii town one can see the myriad businesses run by all communities from Kenya. Some of this growth can be attributed to the remittances from the Kisiis in the diaspora.

Kisiis are also famous for their beautiful soap stone carvings, which earn a considerable income for the women and young men. The soap stone is found in the Tabaka hills of Western Kenya, near the town of Kisii. A soft and easily worked stone, it comes in a variety of colours ranging from cream and lavender to black.

KISII

Obukima Bwobore

Ingredients

3 cups millet grains
1 cup dried cassava
1 cup wheat flour
1 litre water (approx)

Method

Grind the millet with the traditional stone until the required consistency.
Mix this with dried cassava that has been ground and the wheat flour.
The wheat flour makes it smoother.
Boil enough water depending on how stiff you want the ugali to get.
Add the flour and let it boil for three minutes before you start mixing it.
Stir it on low heat until its firm for about 10 minutes.
Plate it on an 'ekee' (Kisii thermos like basket) lightly dusted with the flour so that the ugali doesn't stick to the sides.

Serves 3.

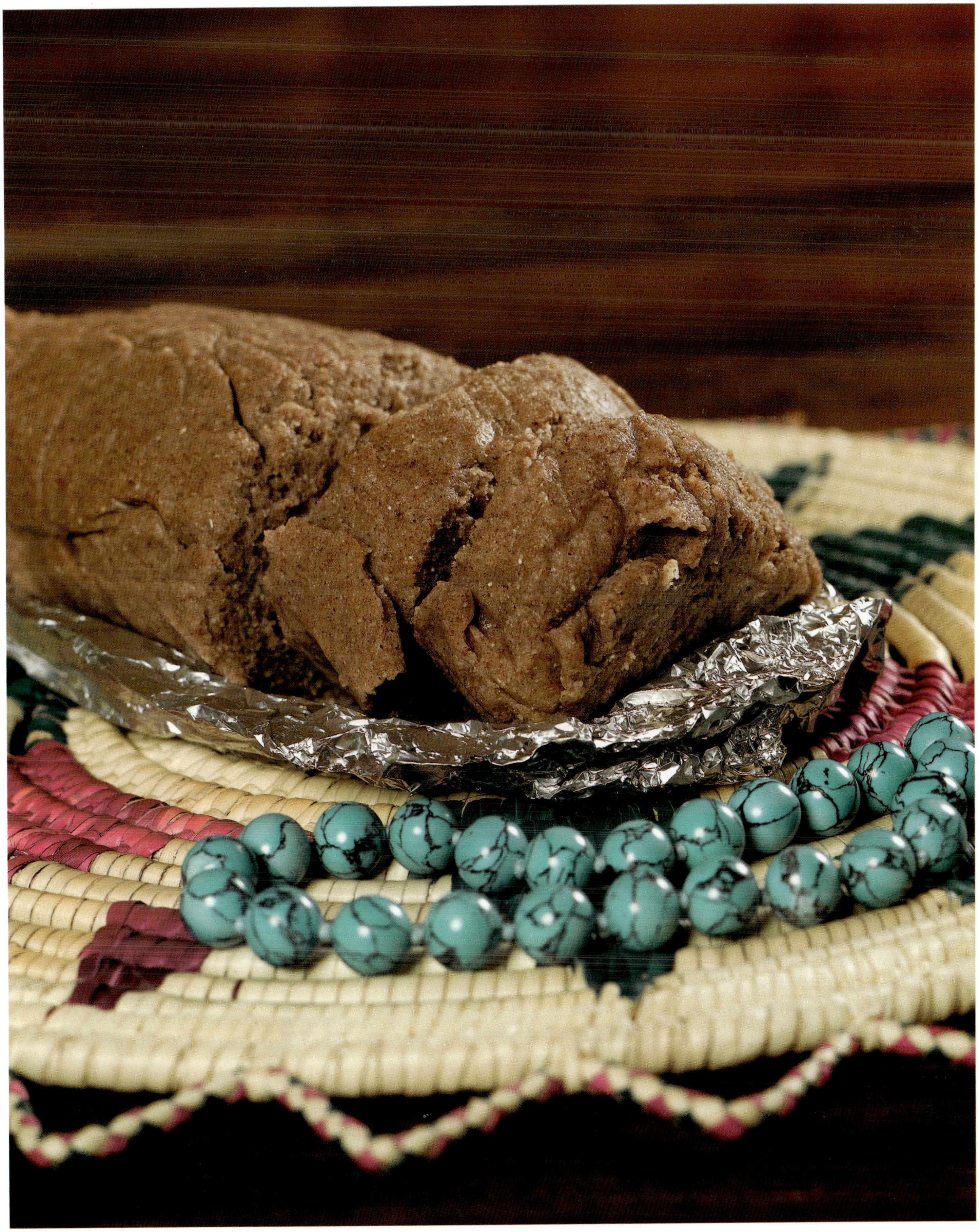

Omutwe we Mburi

KISII

Ingredients

1 whole goat's head
2 litres water
1 onion, chopped
2 tomatoes, chopped
4 cloves of garlic, crushed
2 bunches dania, chopped (coriander)
2 tbsp oil
salt to taste

Method

Roast the goat's head over an open fire then remove the hair.
Wash the head thoroughly and then boil it in water for about 1 hour.
Remove the head and retain the stock.
Remove the meat from the head, including around the jaws and the tongue.
Chop the meat up and fry it in the onions.
Add the tomatoes, garlic and dania then return this mix into its original stock.
Add salt.

This stew is used when someone is recovering from an illness.

Serves 3.

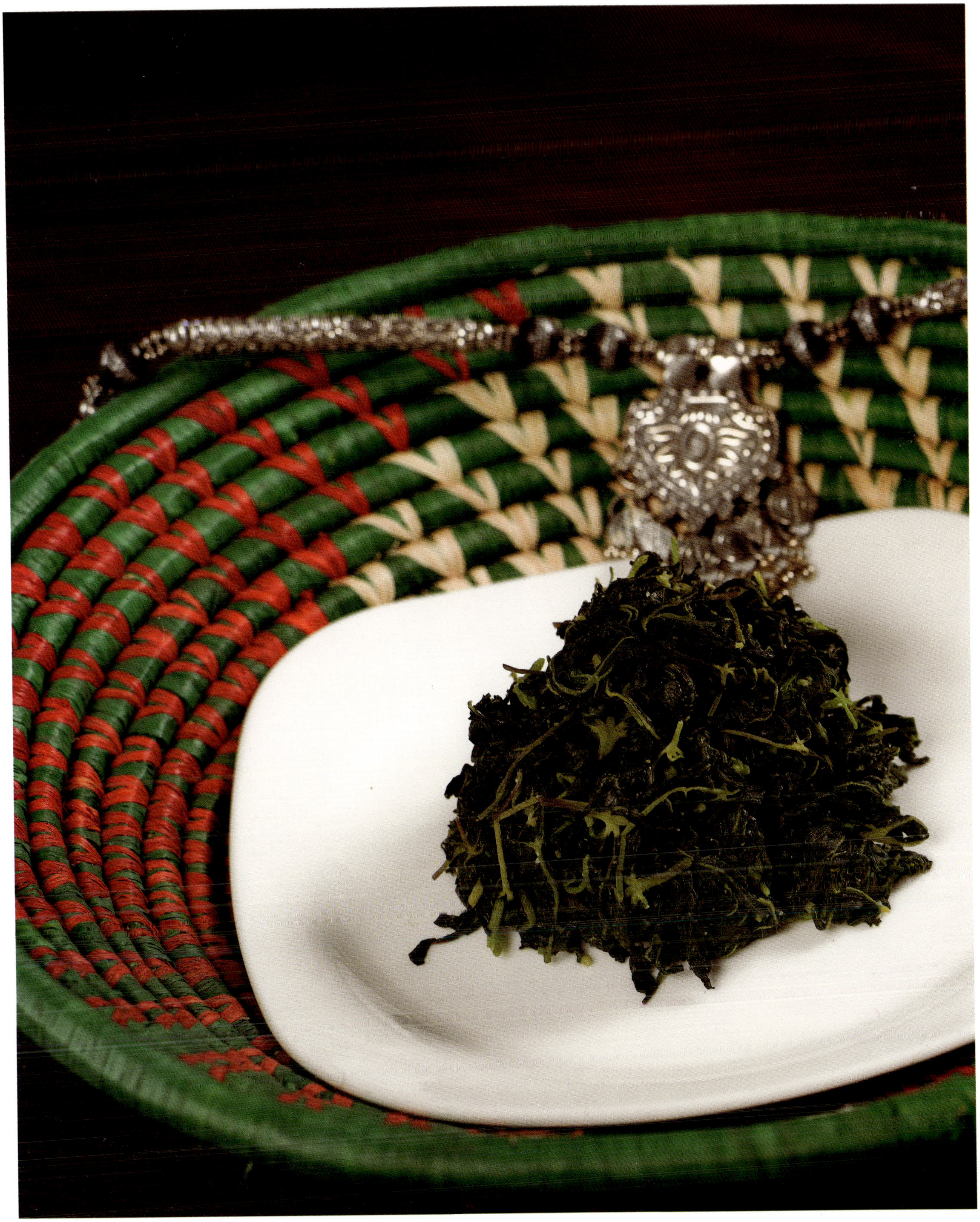

KISII

Omugaye

Ingredients

3 cups green maize kernals
6 green bananas
salt to taste

Method

Boil the green maize and the bananas separately until cooked and soft. Mix them together and mash them with salt.

Serves 3.

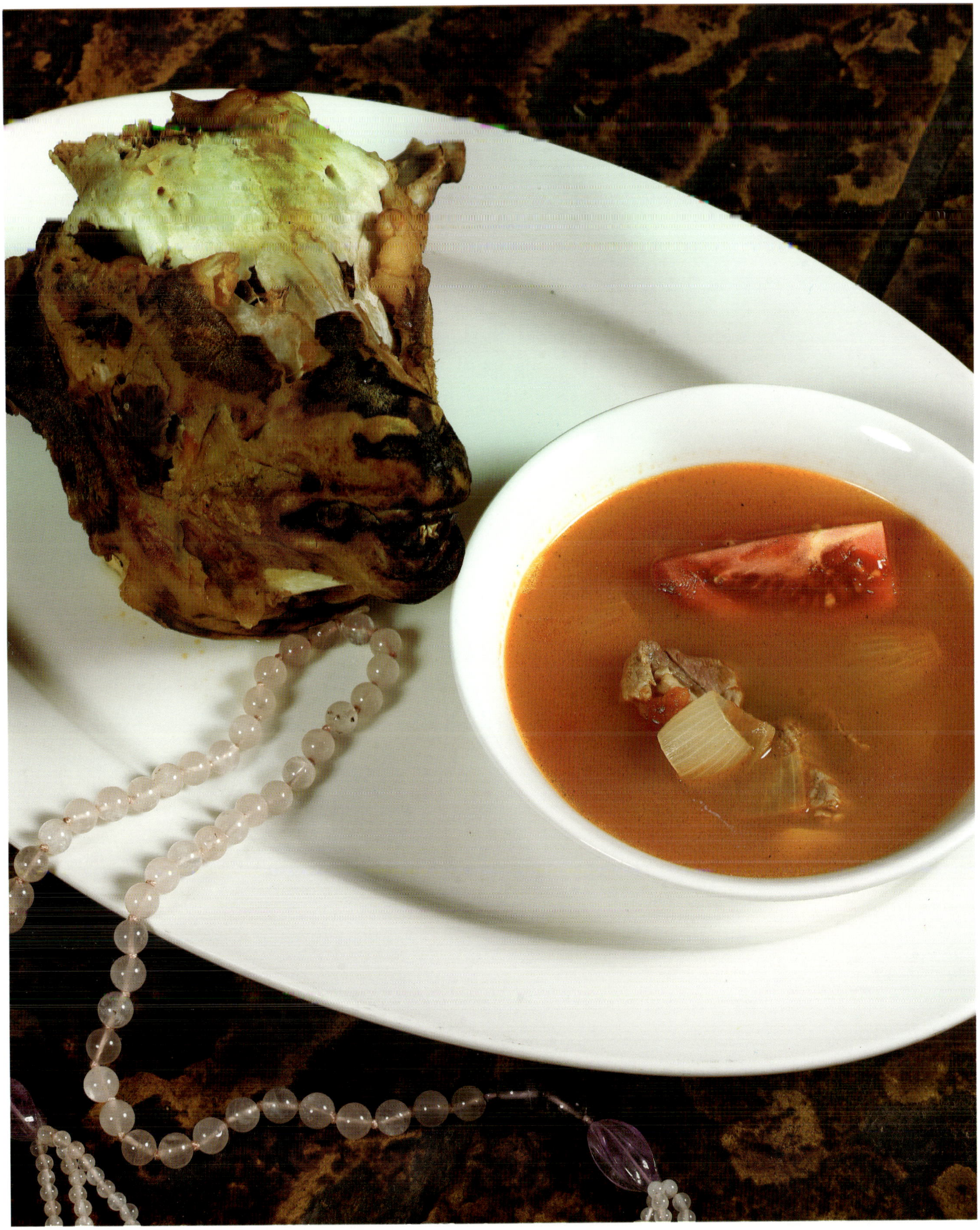

KISII

Sagaa

Ingredients

salt to taste
5 bunches sagaa (spider plant leaves)
little water

Method

Ensure that you wash the vegetables very well. Boil water with salt in it and then add the vegetables.

Sagaa is great for breastfeeding mums.

Serves 4.

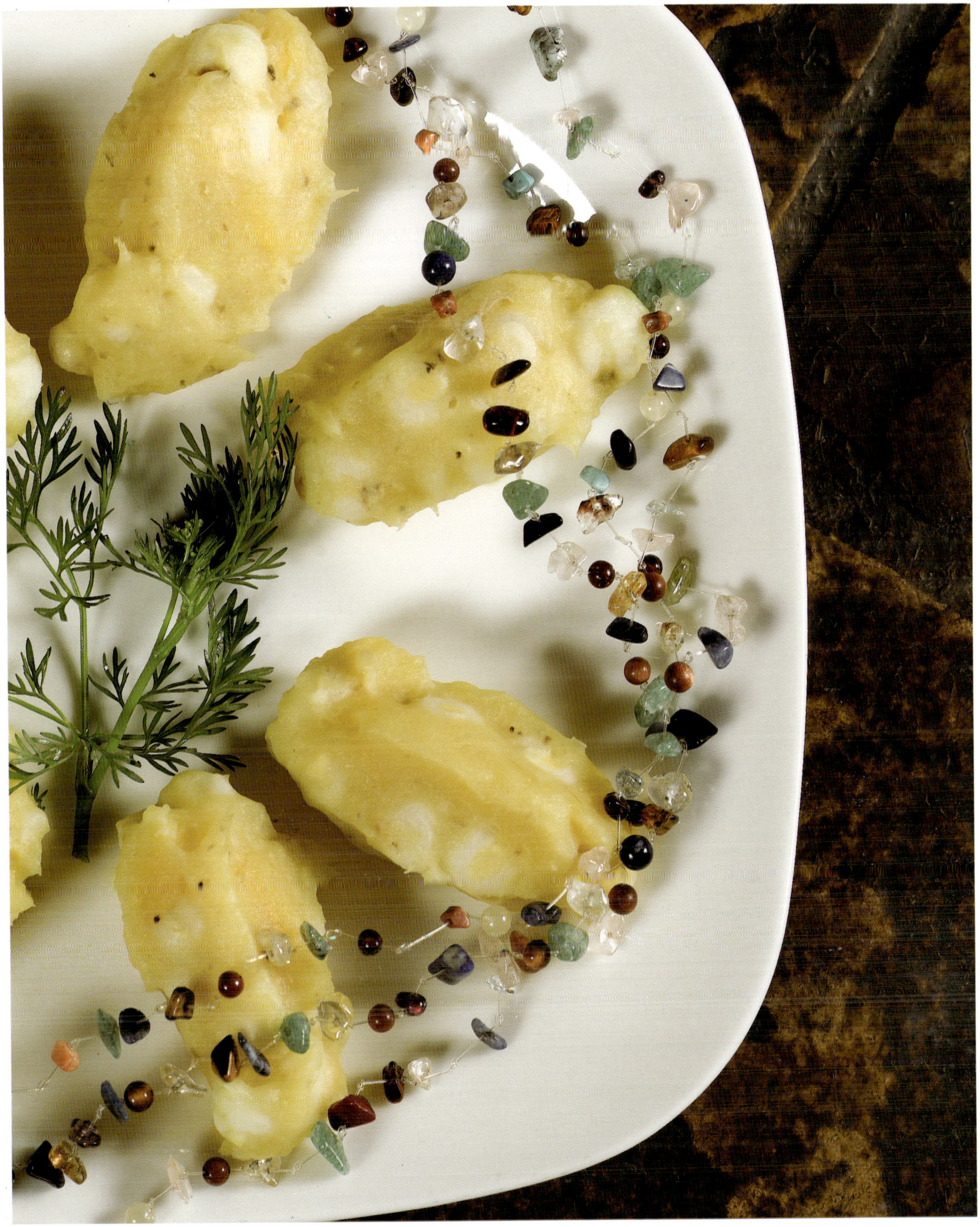

82

Luhya

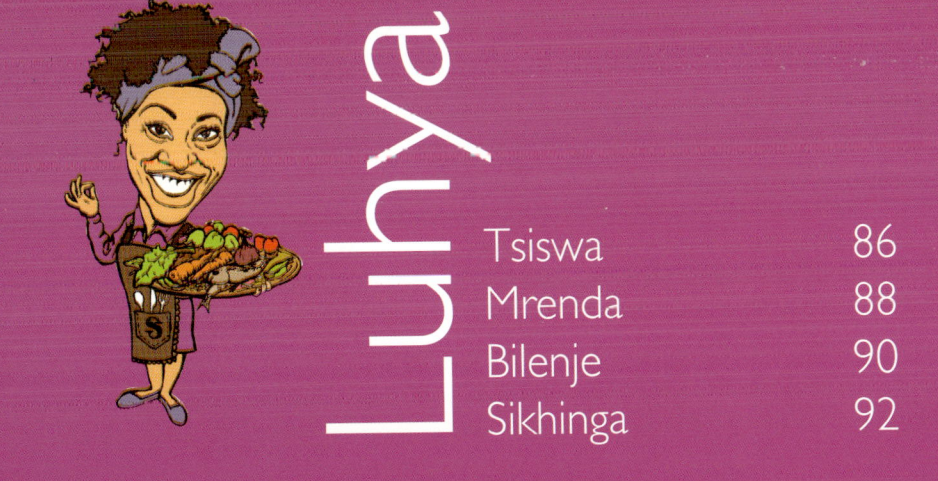

Tsiswa	86
Mrenda	88
Bilenje	90
Sikhinga	92

Lilac breasted roller.
This bird is found in the eastern and southern africa and turns heads with its conspicuous, colourful plumage - its throat is lilac, its belly is light blue and the underside of its wingtips is a brilliant royal blue. With this colouration, the lilac breasted roller is considered one of the most beautiful birds in the world.

Isukha warrior

The Luhya tribe is a Bantu tribe living in Kenya's agriculturally fertile Western region. Though considered one tribe, the Luhya consists of over 18 sub tribes; Bukusu, Maragoli, Banyala, Banyore, Matsotso, Gisu, Idakho, Isukha, Kabras, Khayo, Kisa, Marachi, Marama, Masaaba, Samia, Tachoni, Tiriki and Wanga.

Traditionally the extended clan was at the centre of the Luhya culture. They practiced polygamy, and a man was given more respect depending on the number of wives he had. This is because only a very wealthy man could afford to pay the dowry for several wives. Today, polygamy is no longer widely practiced, but dowry payment is still honored in some Luhya communities.

Traditional male circumcision is an important ritual in most Luhya sub tribes and still takes place every August and December. Circumcision marks the initiation from boyhood to manhood.

Luhya people are great sports enthusiasts, especially when it comes to rugby and soccer. Traditional bull fighting is still considered a sport among sections of the Luhya ethnic groups.

One of the most common myths among the Luhya group relates to the origin of the Earth and human beings. According to this myth, Were (God) first created Heaven, then Earth. The Earth created by Were had three types of soil: top soil, which was black; intermediate soil, which was red; and bottom soil, which was white. From the black soil, Were created a black man; from the red soil, he created a brown man; and from the white soil, he created a white man.

Kakamega Forest National Reserve is the only tropical rainforest in Kenya and is twice the size of Nairobi National Park. The forest has been protected since 1933 and includes some of Africa's greatest hard and soft woods. Some of the animals one can expect to see include leopard, Colobus monkey, Olive baboon, Ted Tailed monkey, bushpig, duiker, civet, sunni, clawless otter and porcupine.

LUHYA

Tsiswa

Ingredients

1 cup fresh flying termites
2 tsp oil
salt to taste

Method

Put the live termites in water, which makes them unable to fly away.
Then heat the oil in a pan and fry the termites on low heat until crispy and well done.
Season with salt and eaten as a snack.

During the rainy season termites are trapped by the children using a blanket as they beat the ground with sticks to drive them out.

Serves 2.

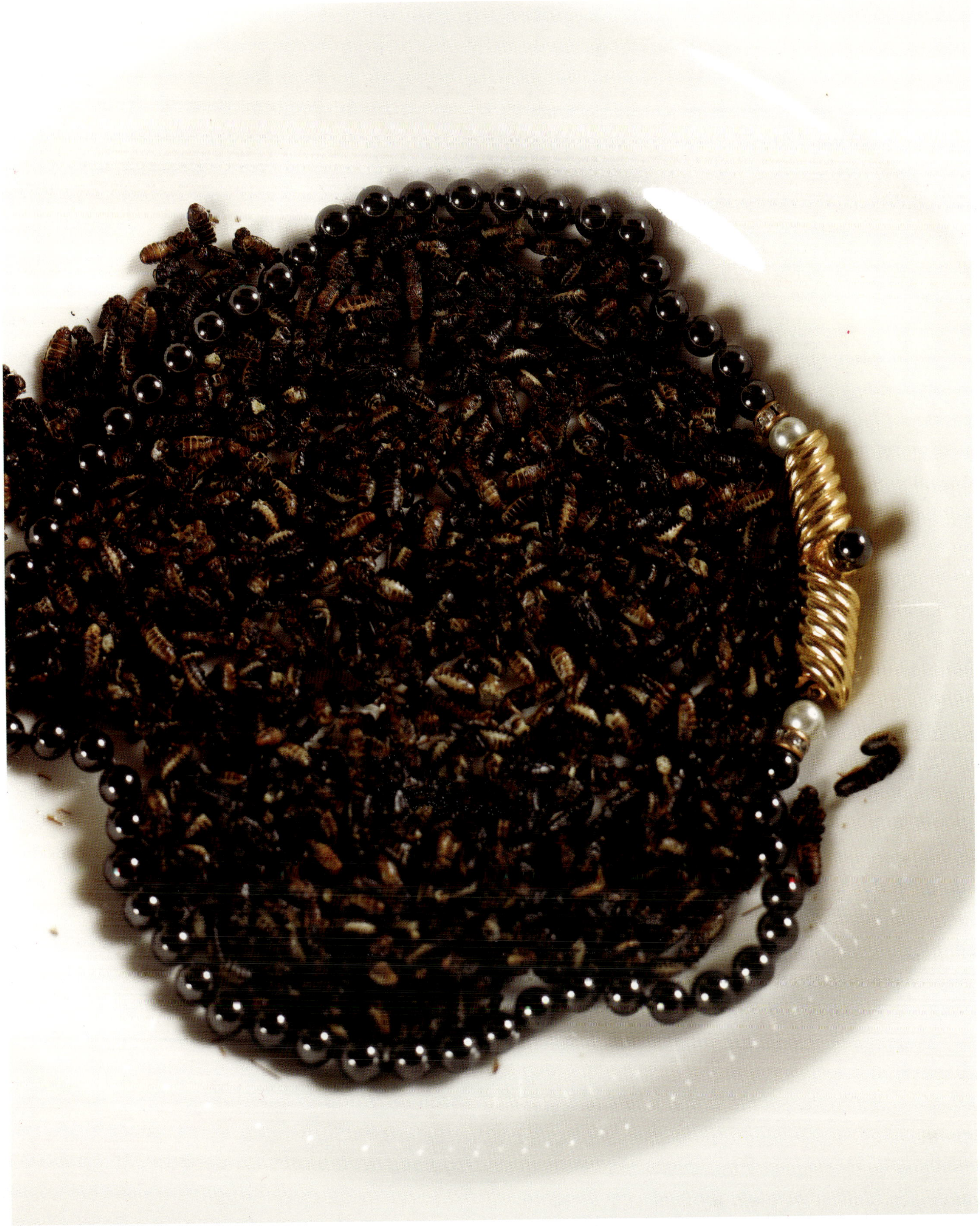

LUHYA

Mrenda

Ingredients

3 bunches mrenda (jute leaves)
1 tsp traditional magadi ash (bicarbonate of soda)
salt to taste

Method

After removing the leaves from the stem, wash carefully.
Boil water in a non-aluminium pot and add ash to the water.
The ash preserves the colour and also acts as a tenderizer.
Put the vegetables into the boiling water and cover the pot for 30 minutes until tender and not bitter.
Season and serve hot with ugali.

Serves 3.

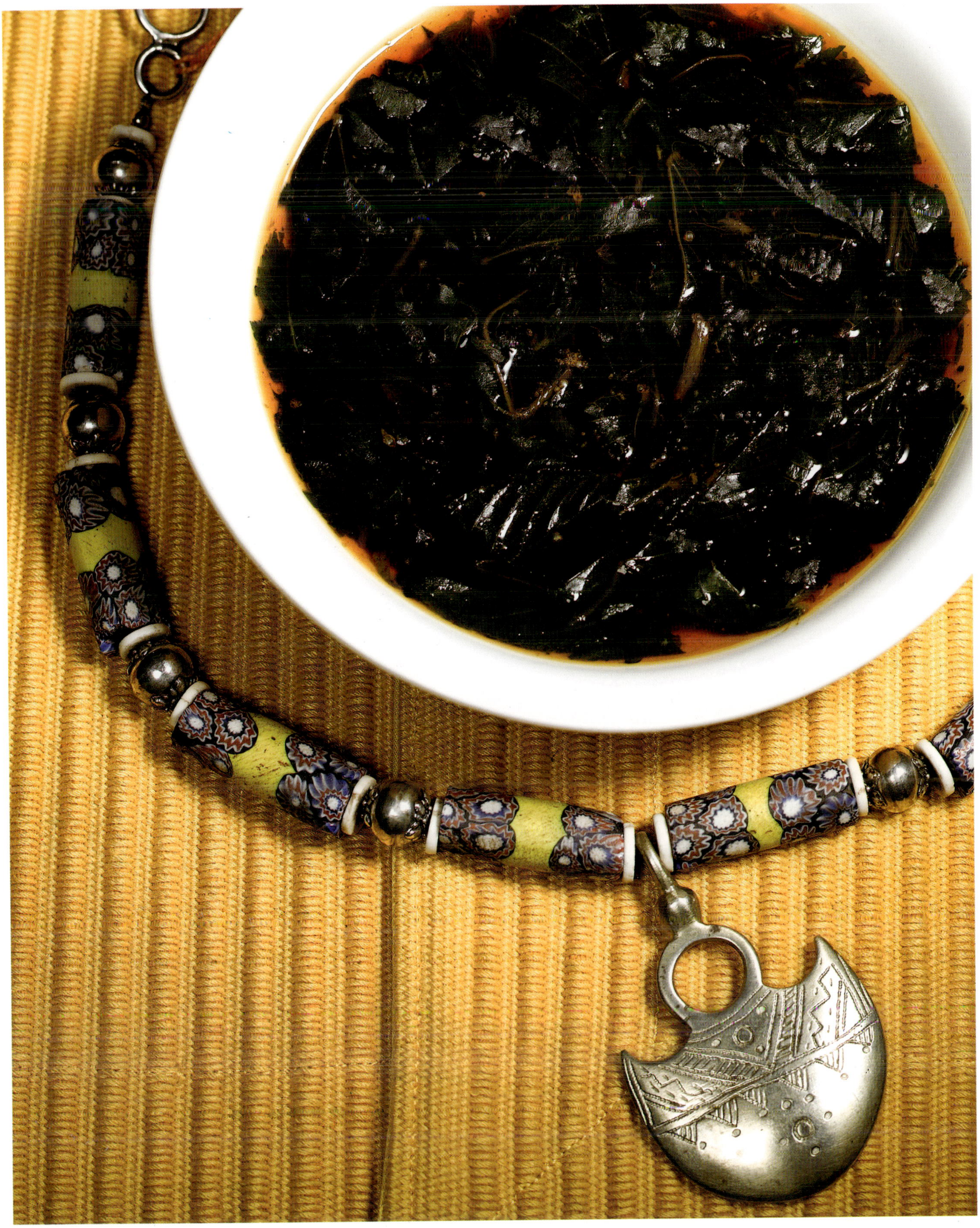

LUHYA

Bilenje

Ingredients

4 cow's feet
salt to taste

Method

Cut off the nails from the cow's feet and then burn off the cow's fur in an open fire, scrape it off cleanly. Boil the feet in plenty of water until tender (4-6 hours) and then season with salt.
The soup can be drunk on its own and the meat eaten off the feet.

Serves 4.

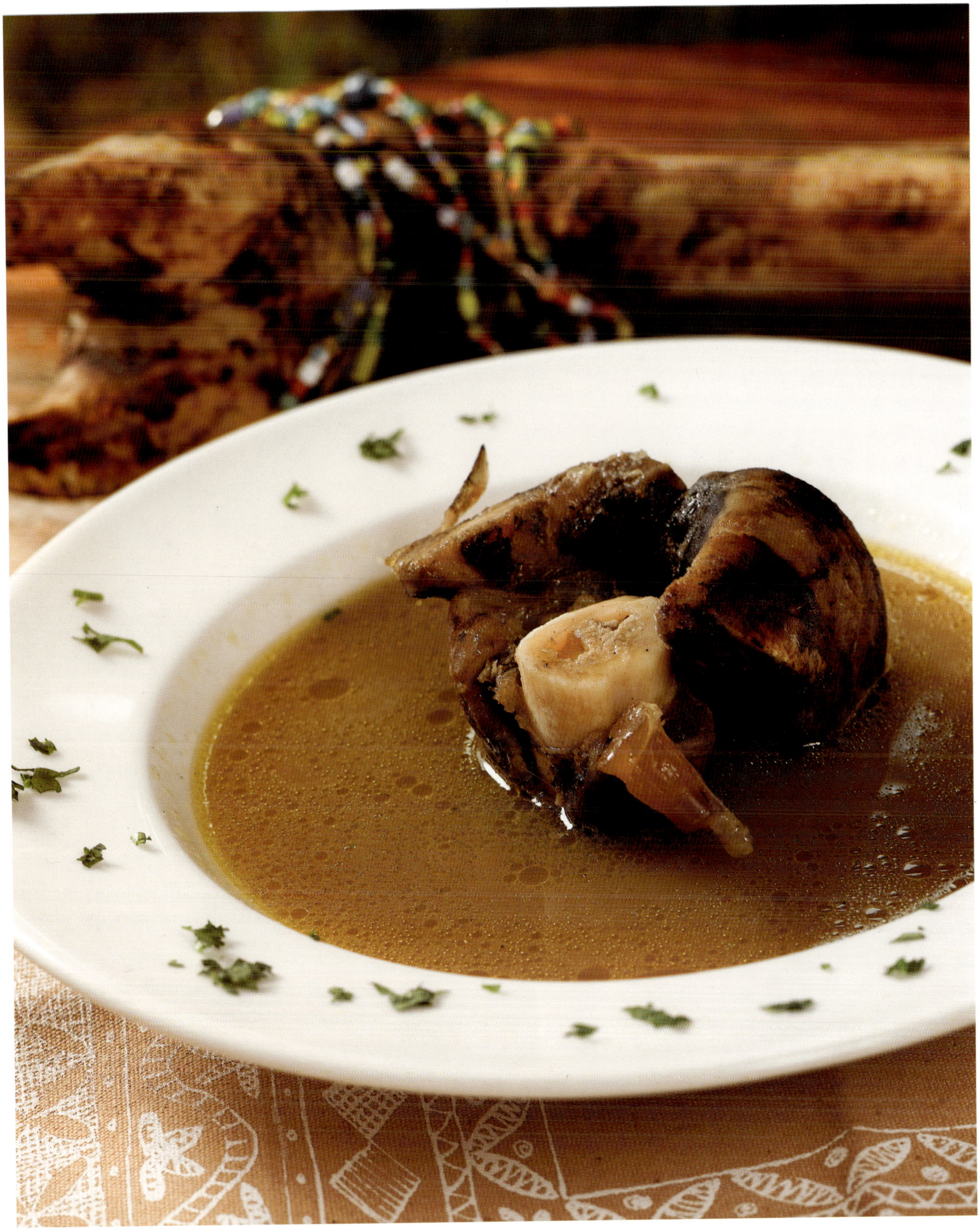

LUHYA

Sikhinga

Ingredients

1kg oxtail cut into segments
4 onions, chopped
6 cloves of garlic, crushed
2 inch ginger, crushed
2 bunches dania, chopped
little oil

Method

Boil the oxtail for two hours or until tender.
Put 2 onions into this water so that you can get soup from this first step of the recipe. Set aside.
Fry 2 onions, the garlic and ginger and then add the meat with little or no oil as oxtail has too much oil.
When the meat has absorbed the onion flavour, add dhania and serve.

Serves 3.

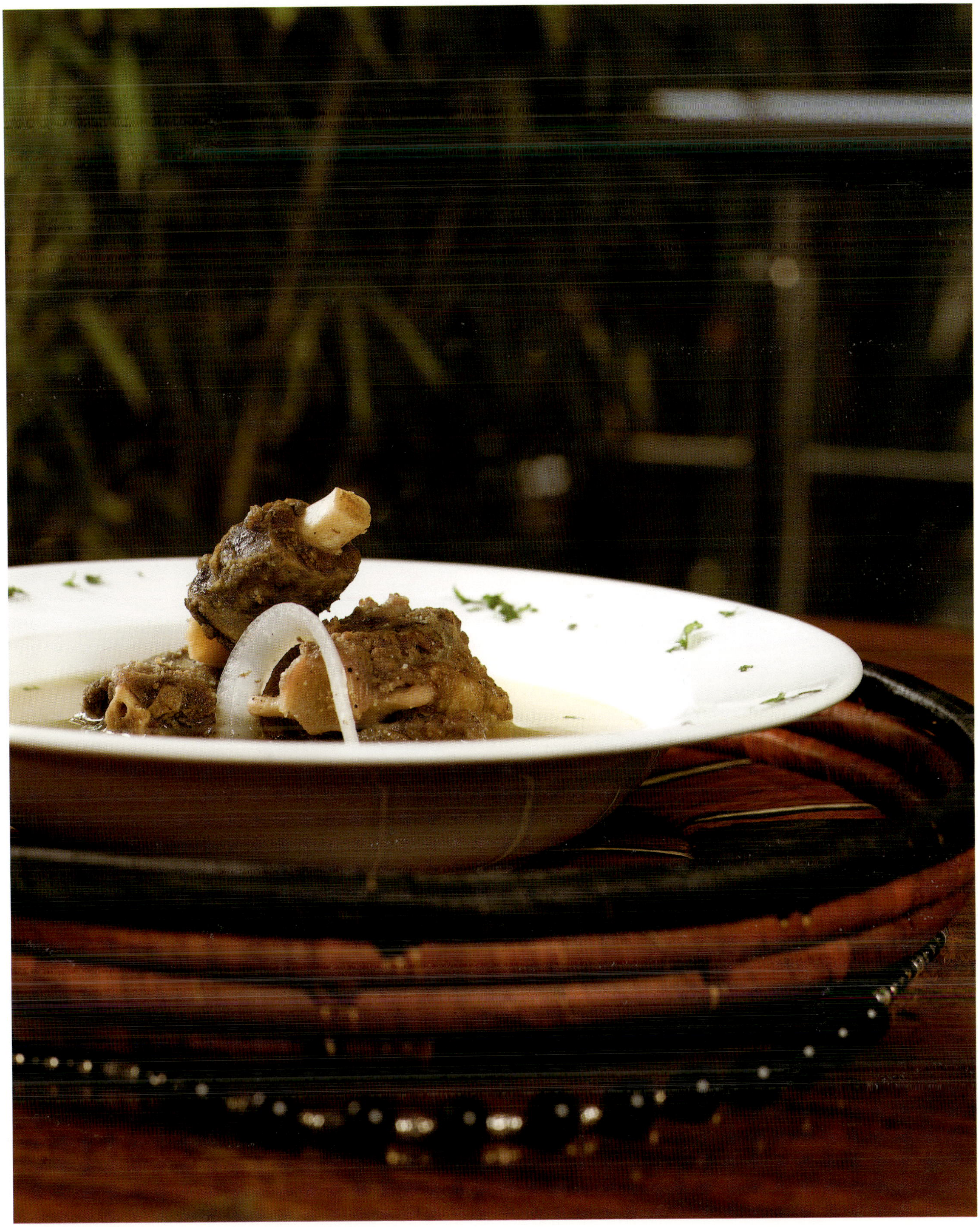

Kisumu.
This port city lies on the north eastern shore of Lake Victoria. It is the third-largest city in Kenya with about 320,000 people. Kisumu is an important trading centre for the region's agricultural products. The humid climate rusts the tin roofs on the huts in this very densely settled area.

Luo

Aluru	98
Sukuma Osuga mix	100
Oodol	102
Aliya	104

Luo man in ngoma outfit

The Luo community lives primarily in the area surrounding Lake Victoria. They are fun loving people who enjoy a good meal and their staple food is maize meal (ugali) and fish. Their area is not considered high potential for producing staple crops such as maize, potatoes or beans although in some parts of the plains, they grow rice.

The most interesting thing about the Luo is that the women play the primary role in farming. It is basically an activity to put food on the table and not necessarily to make money. Fishing is the real income earner. Outside Luoland, the Luo comprise a significant fraction of East Africa's intellectual and skilled labour force in various professions.

Traditionally, music was the most widely practiced art in the Luo community. At any time of the day or night, some music was being made. Music was not made for its own sake it was functional. It was used for ceremonial, religious, political, or incidental purposes. Music was performed during funerals (Tero buru), to praise the departed, to console the bereaved, to keep people awake at night, to express pain and agony, and was also used during cleansing and chasing away of spirits.

Music was also played during ceremonies like beer parties (Dudu, ohangla dance), welcoming back the warriors from a war, during a wrestling match (Olengo), during courtship, etc. Work songs also existed. These were performed both during communal work like building, weeding, etc. and individual work like pounding of cereals, or winnowing. Music was also used for ritual purposes like chasing away evil spirits (nyawawa), who visit the village at night, in rain making, and during divinations and healing.

The Luo music was shaped by the total way of life, lifestyles, and life patterns of individuals of this community. Because of that, the music had characteristics which distinguished it from the music of other communities. This can be seen, heard, and felt in their melodies, rhythms, mode of presentation and dancing styles, movements, and formations. It can also be seen in the crowds drawn to the dance halls who enjoy this music

LUO

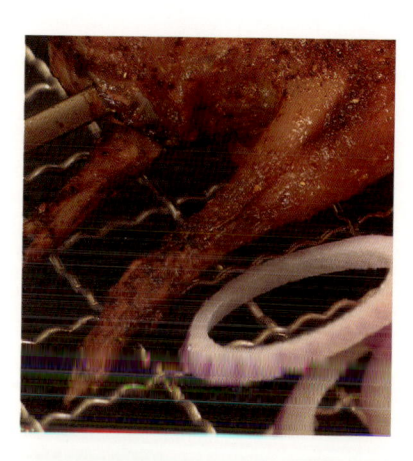

Aluru

Ingredients

2 onions, chopped
salt to taste
3 tbsp oil
5 whole quail

Method

Break the necks of the birds then roast them over an open fire.
This makes it easier to remove the feathers.
Then remove the internal organs.
Dry them in the sun after rubbing them with salt.
Then boil them for about 2 hours.
Fry them in the onions.

These are small birds (quail) trapped in a sigol (pole) that is tied with 10 to 20 live birds. The bird that cries the most is put at the top of the sigol so that it can draw others into the trap. It has traps at the bottom made of cow's tail. One must buy the birds alive, and they must reach home alive. This is a Luo delicacy.

Serves 5.

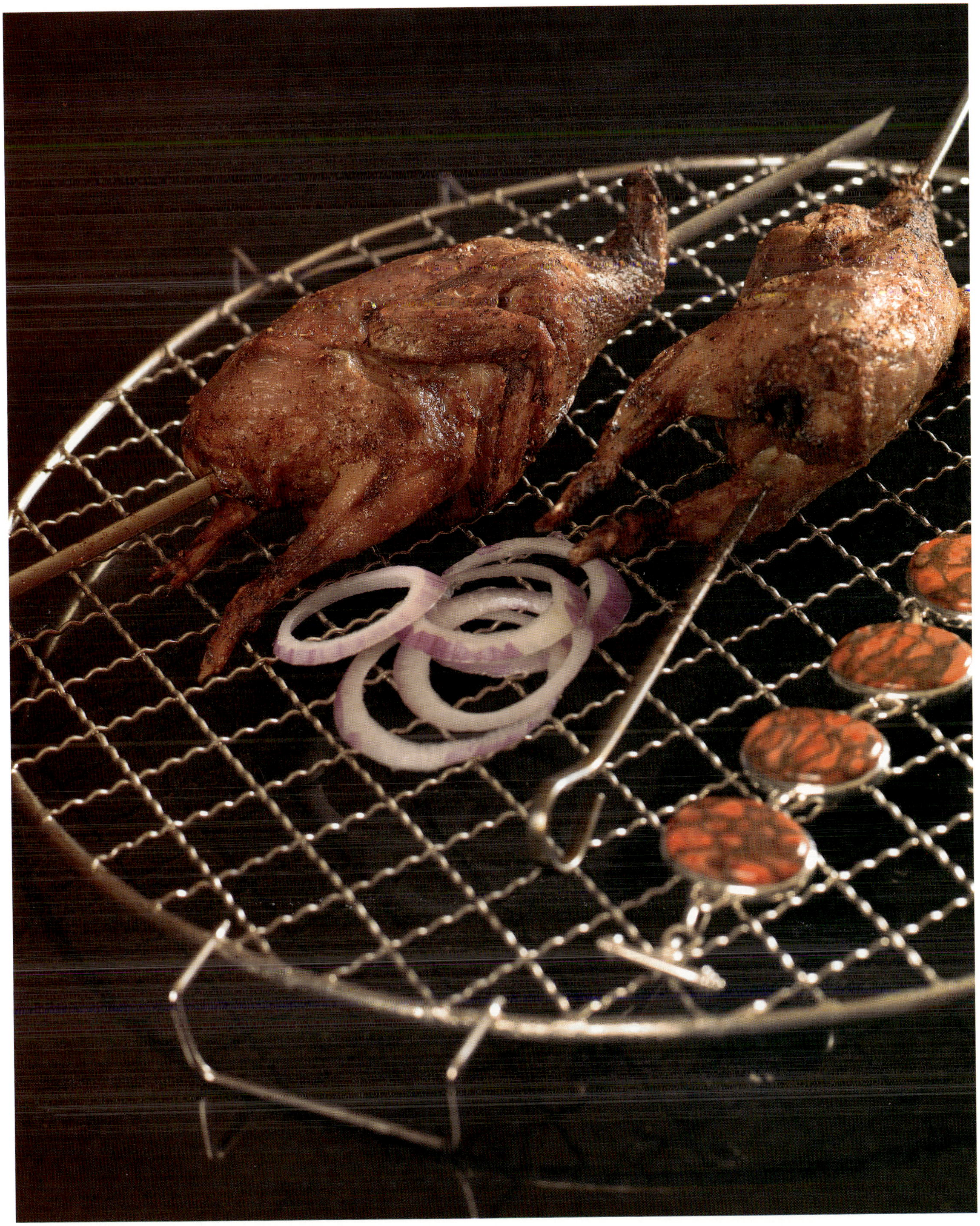

LUO

Sukuma Osuga Mix

Ingredients

3 bunches sukuma wiki (kale leaves)
5 bunches osuga (blacknight shade leaves)
1 onion, chopped
2 tbsp oil
salt to taste
1 cup whipped fresh cream

Method

Thoroughly wash the Osuga and then cut into the desired size.
Boil them for one hour and then pour out that water because it is bitter.
Keep this overnight.
The next day, boil the Osuga in milk for about 20 minutes.
Do this every day for about 5 days until it is no longer bitter, then add salt.
Thoroughly wash the sukuma wiki, and then cut into the desired size.
Blanch the sukuma wiki for a short time so that it cooks faster.
Fry the onions in the oil until golden brown then put in the sukuma wiki.
Let it cook until almost ready then add whipped cream just five minutes before you switch off the fire.
You may combine this with the cooked osuga.

Serves 3.

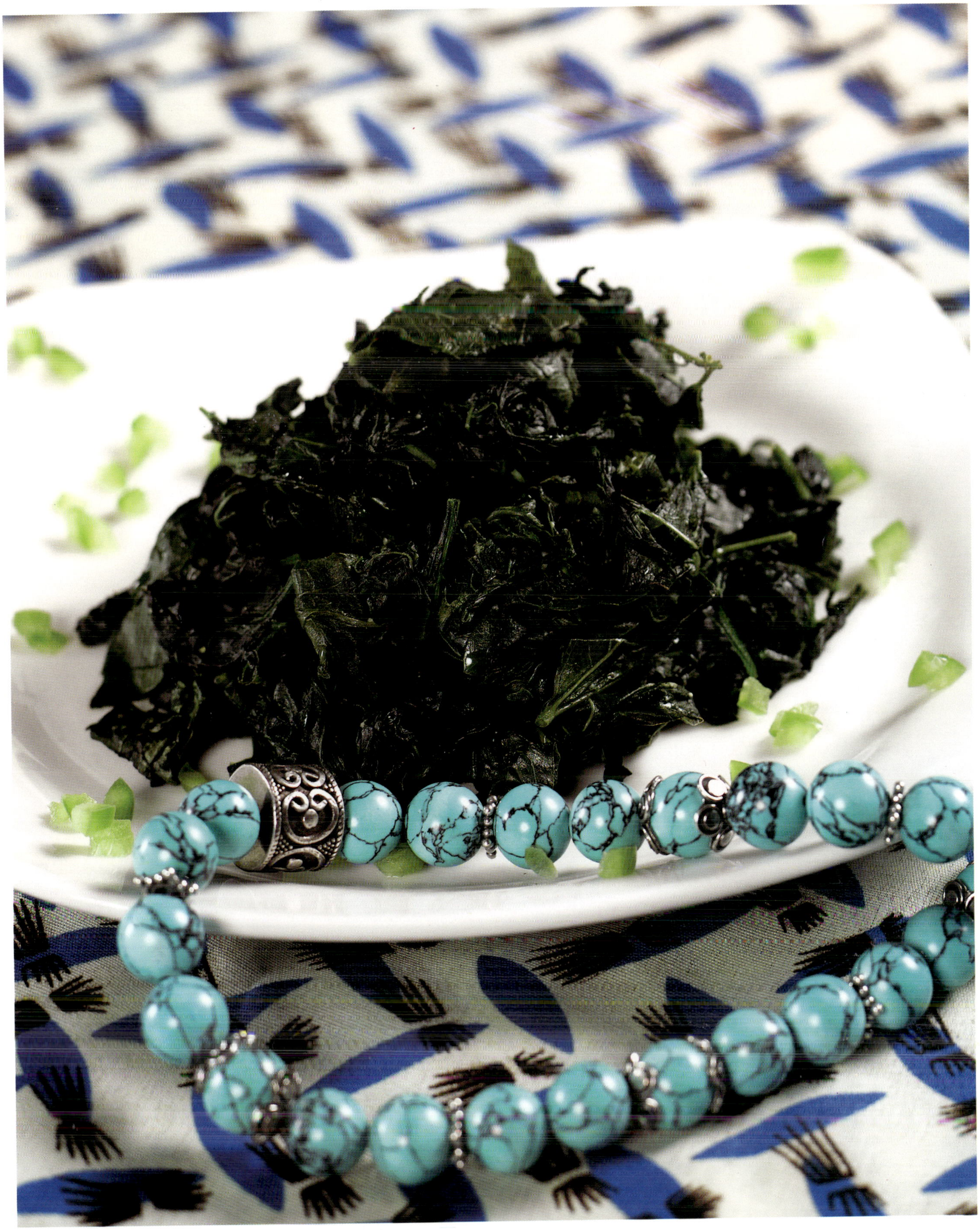

LUO

Oodol

Ingredients

2 smoked mud fish (oodol meaning folded as the fish is sold folded and smoked)
½ cup oil
4 tomatoes, diced
2 red onions, chopped
2 pinches of thutho (magadi ash)

Method

Heat the oil in a frying pan and fry the onions until golden in colour.
Add in the tomatoes and cook until they collapse.
Add the smoked fish, that must be soaked for at least 30 minutes before preparing.
Cook then add in the thutho.
Simmer for 10 minutes and serve hot with brown wimbi (millet) ugali.

Serves 2.

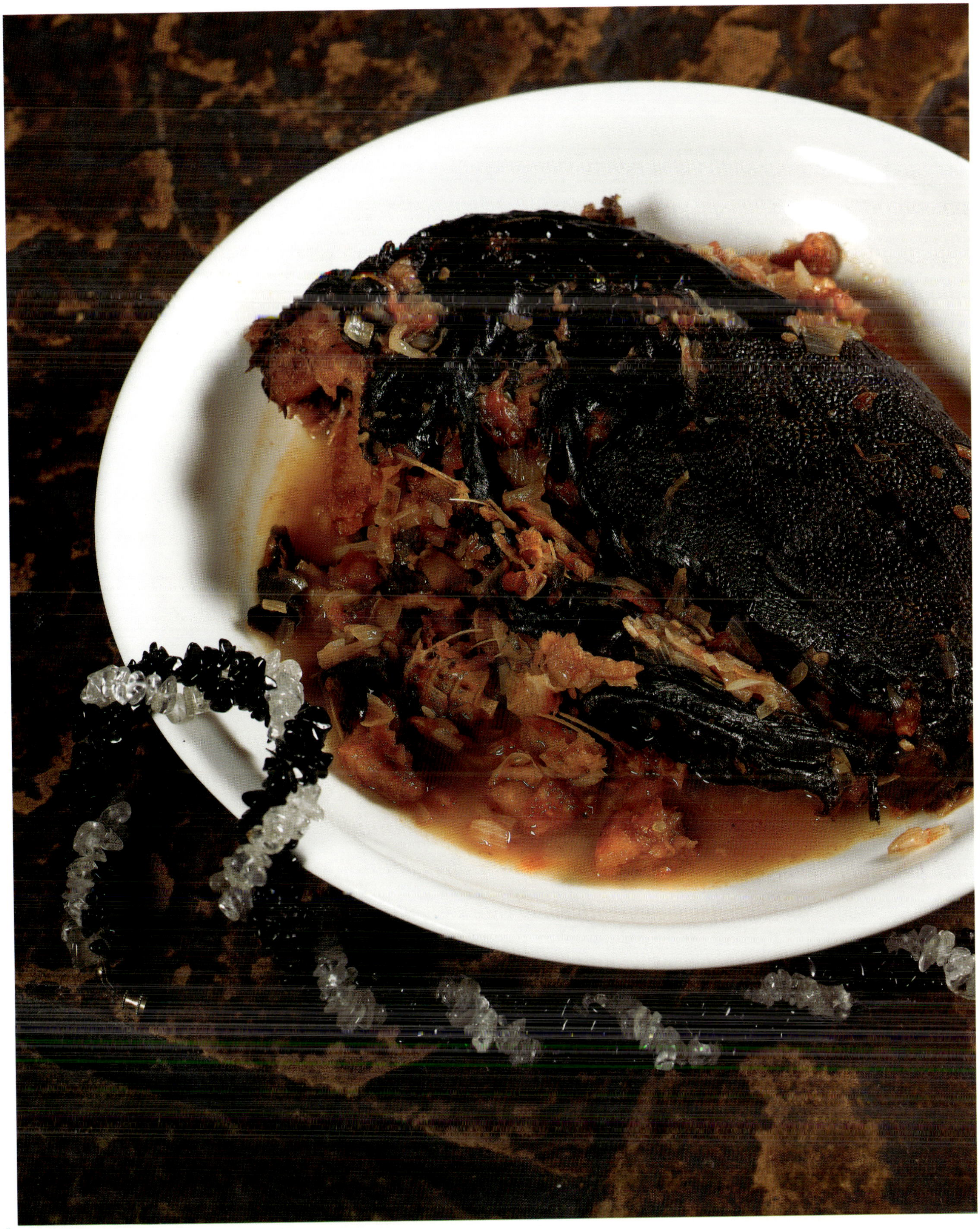

LUO

Aliya

Ingredients

1½ kg beef steak
2 onions, chopped
2 tsp oil
salt to taste
2 tomatoes, chopped
½ cup fresh milk

Method

Cut steak (beef) into strips and rub them in salt
Sun-dry these strips for between 2 weeks and 1 month.
{A short cut is to roast the beef and then sun dry it for a shorter time}
Cut it into cubes and then boil it until it's soft.
Then fry it with onions, tomatoes and a little fresh milk.
This recipe can also work well with game meat.

Serves 4.

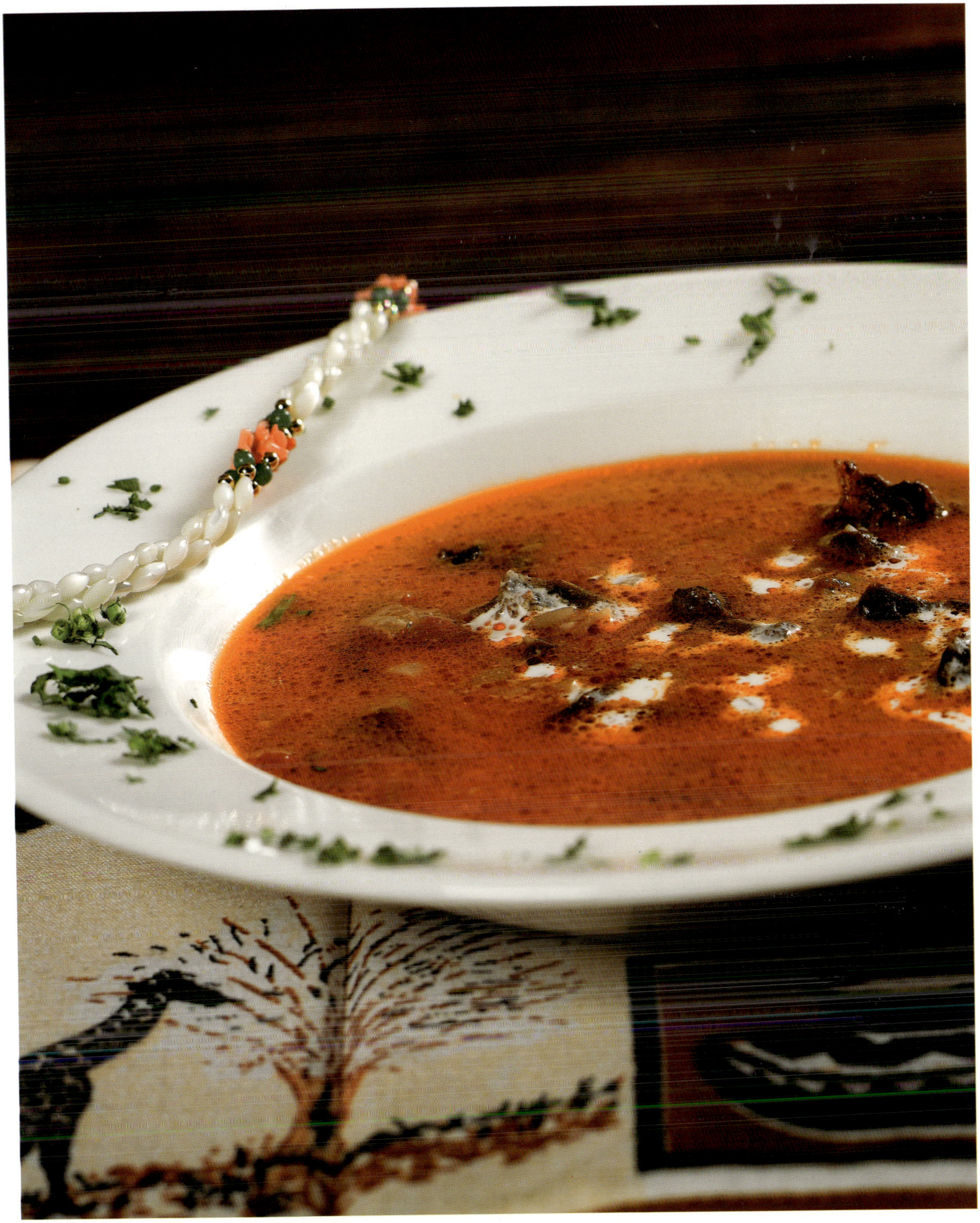

106

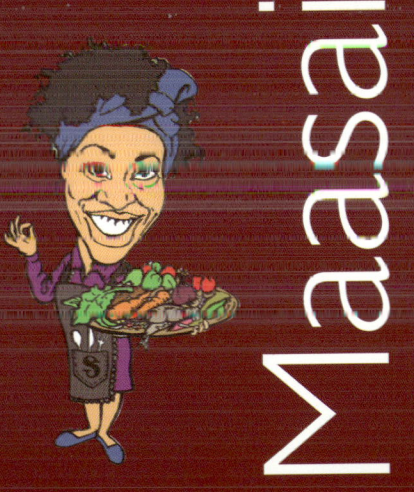

Maasai

Rongera 110
Ole Naotho 112
Mururi 114

Lake Natron.
The northern headwaters of this lake border Tanzania in southern Kenya. Lake Natron is the world's most famous alkaline lake. It lies at the foot of the Ol Doinyo Lengai volcano. Saline or alkaline lakes are known for their high pH combined with high salinity. The lake is also home to millions of flamingos and pelicans.

Young Maasai married woman

The Maasai community is a unique and popular one due to their long preserved culture. Despite education, civilization and western cultural influences, the Maasai have clung to their traditional way of life, making them a symbol of Kenyan culture. Maasais speak Maa, a Nilotic ethnic language from their origin in the Nile region of North Africa.

Tragedy struck the Maasai tribe at the turn of the century. An epidemic of deadly diseases attacked and killed large numbers of the Maasai's animals. This was quickly followed by severe drought that lasted years. Over half of the Maasais and their animals perished during this period. Soon after, more than two thirds of the Maasai's land in Kenya was taken away by the British and the Kenyan government to create both ranches for settlers and Kenya and Tanzania's wildlife reserves and national parks.

The warrior is of great importance as a source of pride in the Maasai culture. To be a Maasai is to be born into one of the world's last great warrior cultures. From boyhood to adulthood, young Maasai boys begin to learn the responsibilities of being a man (helder) and a warrior. The role of a warrior is to protect their animals from human and animal predators, to build kraals (Maasai homes) and to provide security to their families.

Since the Maasai lead a semi-nomadic life, their houses are loosely constructed and semi-permanent. They are usually small, circular houses built by the women using mud, grass, wood and cow-dung.

The Maasai tribe has a deep, almost sacred, relationship with cattle. They are guided by a strong belief that God created cattle especially for them and that they are the sole custodians of all the cattle on earth. This bond has led them into a nomadic way of life following patterns of rainfall over vast land in search of food and water for their large herds of cattle.

Though they traditionally dressed in animal skins, today, typical Maasai dress consists of red sheets, (shuka), wrapped around the body and loads of beaded jewelry placed around the neck and arms. These are worn by both men and women and may vary in colour depending on the occasion. Ear piercing and the stretching of earlobes are also part of Maasai beauty, and both men and women wear metal hoops on their stretched earlobes. Women shave their heads and remove two middle teeth on the lower jaw (for oral delivery of traditional medicine). Many Maasai practice nomadic pastoralism, while others have been absorbed into modern day jobs such as working in tourism where they showcase their culture.

MAASAI

Rongera

Ingredients

2 kg lamb cubes
1 litre osarge (fresh blood)

Method

Cut out cubes of meat from the sheep's neck (it's a delicacy because of the fat).
Steam the meat with half a cup of water for 10 minutes.
When it's cooked and all the water has dried up remove it from the fire.
Add the osarge to the meat and stir.
Serve as a warm biting (eaten only by men).

Serves 4.

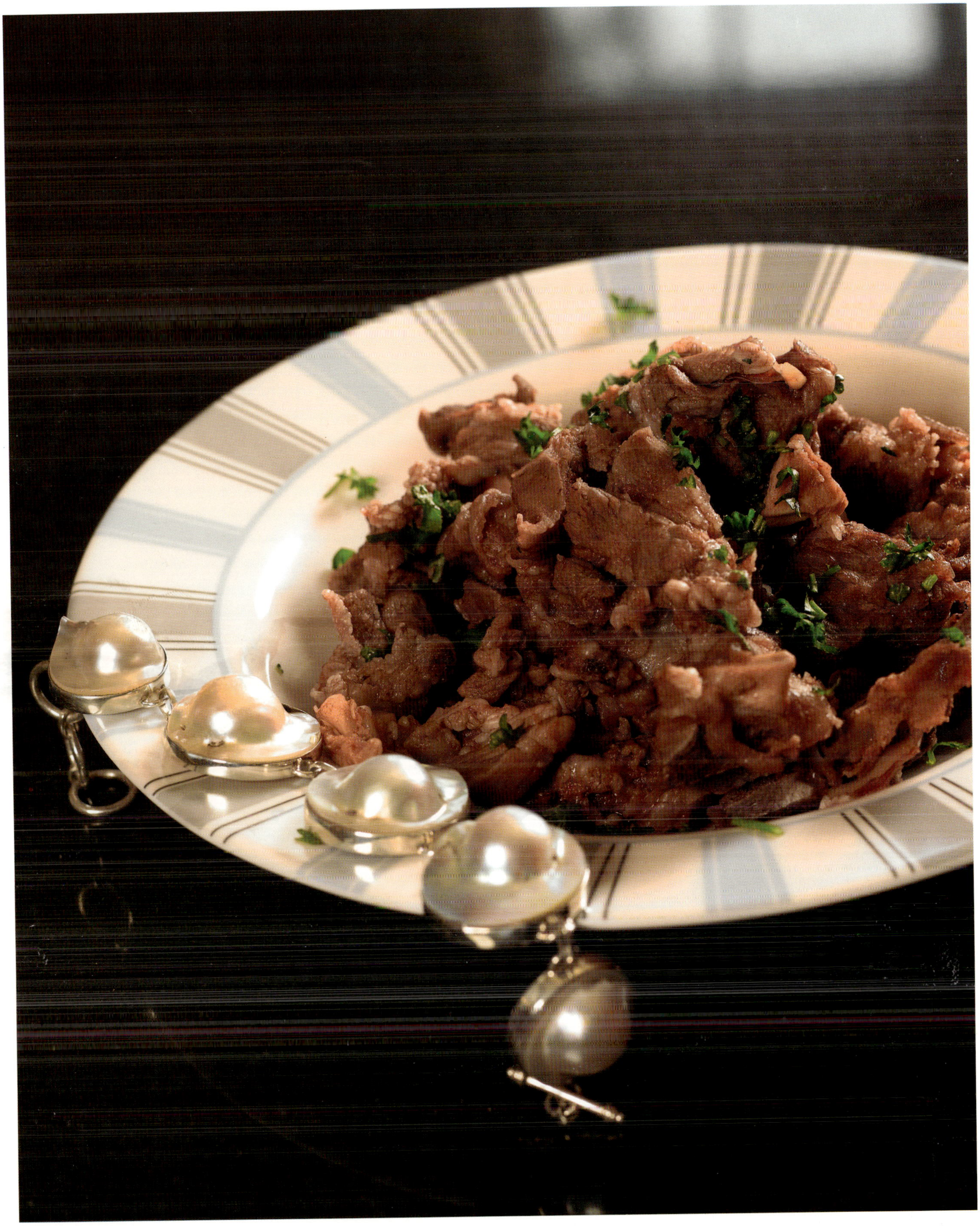

MAASAI

Ole Naotho

Ingredients

1 litre fresh cow's milk

Method

Take cows' milk and put it in a gourd for 5 days, shaking regularly.
Eat it with ugali.

The Maasai never used to boil their milk and this recipe would not work with processed milk.
This is the most common meal among the Maasai as opposed to meat, which was only eaten during special occasions or when an animal was sick.

Serves 3.

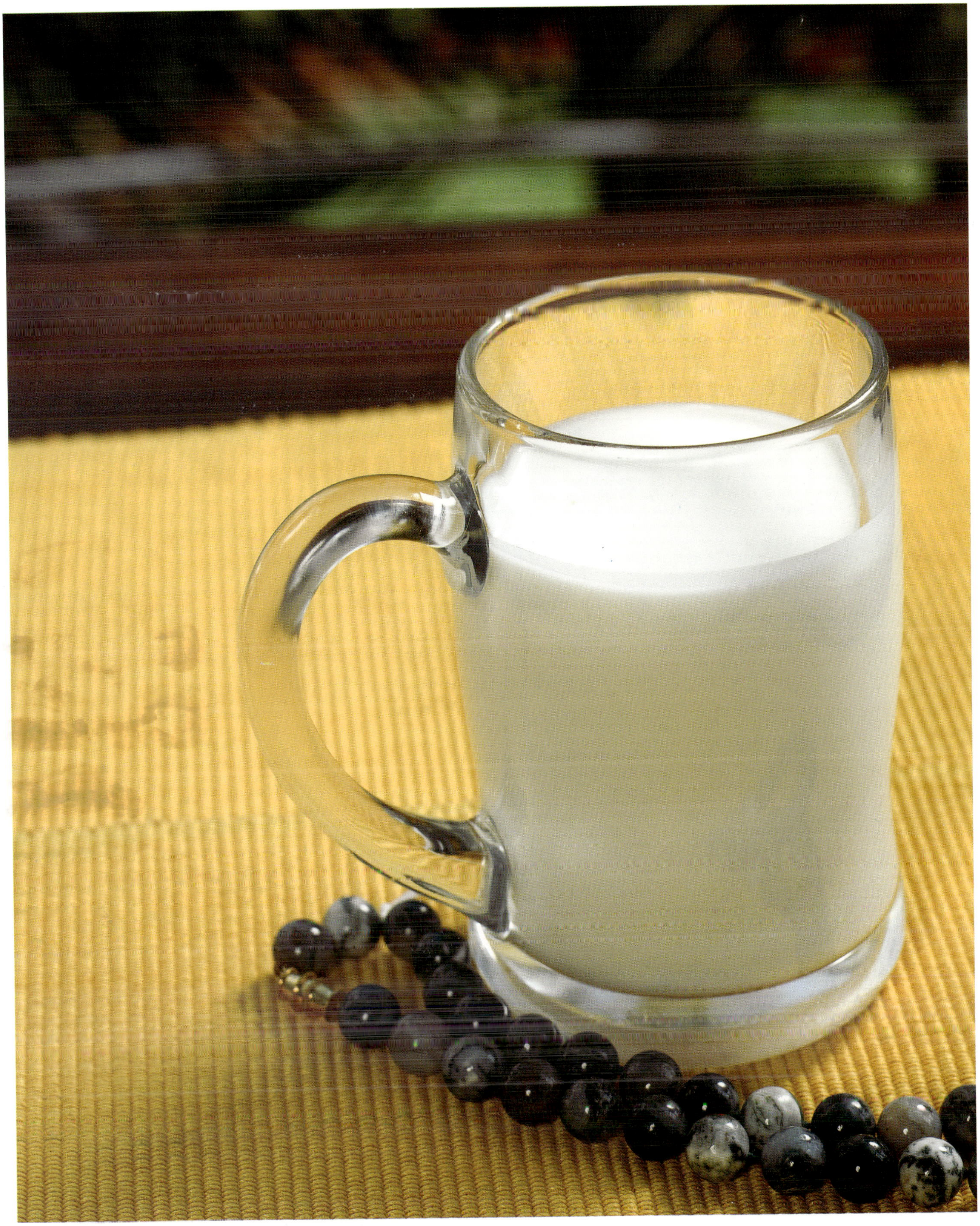

MAASAI

Mururi

Ingredients

2 kg beef cubes
handful maasai herbs & bark

Method

Select a nice portion of beef which has some fat on it.
Boil it for 20 minutes in 2 litres of water.
Remove the meat from the fire and take out the chunks of meat.
Boil the bark mix in the soup for another 20 minutes.
If boiled together with the meat it makes the meat bitter.

Believed to help with digestion and prevent malaria.

Serves 6.

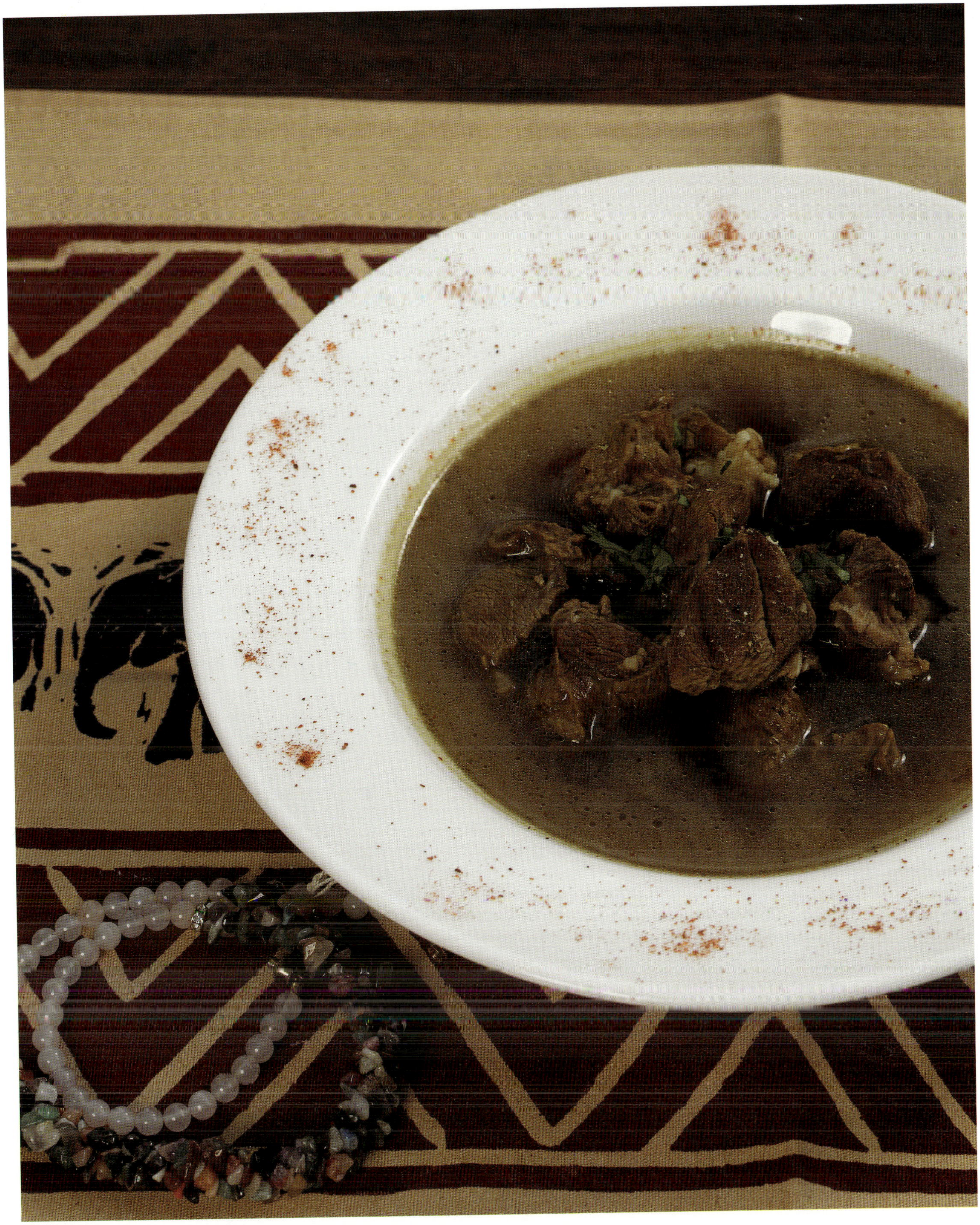

116

Meru

Muree	120
Marigo	122
Njahi	124
Ruguru	126

North of Mount Kenya.
A combine harvester harvests the fields. In addition to wheat, tea, coffee, rice, cotton, and produce are also grown in Kenya. More than three quarters of Kenya's people live from farming. However, only about 12% of Kenya's total land area can be farmed intensively.

Tharaka married woman

The Meru tribe is a Bantu ethnic group who reside on Mount Kenya's agriculturally rich north eastern slope, in the Eastern Province of Kenya. They are divided into seven sub tribes: Tigania, Igembe, Imenti, Miutuni, Igoji, Mwimbi and Muthambi. The Chuka and Tharaka are now considered part of the Meru but they have different oral histories and mythology.

The fertile land produces a large variety of food crops, including staples such as maize, beans, potatoes and millet. Miraa (a stimulant plant) is the most popularly grown cash crop along with coffee, tea and wheat.

The Meru have fairly strict circumcision customs that affect all of life. From the time of circumcision, boys no longer have contact with their mother and girls no longer have contact with their father. A separate house is built for the sons and the mother leaves their food outside the door. This does vary to some degree depending on the level of urban influence, but is still practiced in Meru town. This is one of the major reasons that almost all secondary schools in Meru are boarding schools.

Although society has changed enormously since colonization, a number of important social and cultural traditions remain, either in their original form, or in a shape adapted to modern-day realities. Notable among these is their system of government by a council of elders (Njuri-Ncheke). Also remarkable is the modern version of their female circumcision ceremony, which appears to be gradually gaining ground throughout the population. Called 'Circumcision through Words', the new ceremony almost exactly mirrors the traditional rituals, with the exception that the physical action of cutting has been replaced with symbols and certification. The initiative is supported not only by various women's groups and NGOs, but by the ultra-conservative Njuri-Ncheke themselves.

Taken as a whole, the Meru have one of the most detailed and potentially confusing oral histories of any people in Kenya. It is also one of the most deeply intriguing as it contains extremely strong Biblical similarities that suggest to some that they may once have been one of the Lost Tribes of Israel, and to others that they were once Jewish. This history includes a good part of both Old and New Testament stories: a baby in a basket of reeds who becomes a leader and a prophet, the massacre of newly born babies by an evil king, an exodus, the parting and crossing of the waters by an entire nation, Aaron's Rod in the form of a magic spear or staff, the leadership of a figure comparable to Moses, references to ancient Egypt (Misiri), and so on.

MERU

Muree

Ingredients

8 murwaru bananas (ripe bananas)
20 potatoes, quartered
3 cups cow peas (black-eyed bean)
salt to taste

Method

Grind the cowpeas with a stone so that they are loosely broken.
Then boil them on their own until cooked.
Add the potatoes to the boiling cowpeas.
When these are almost ready, put in your ripe bananas.
Add salt and mash them until smooth.
You can add fresh cream to it.

Serves 5.

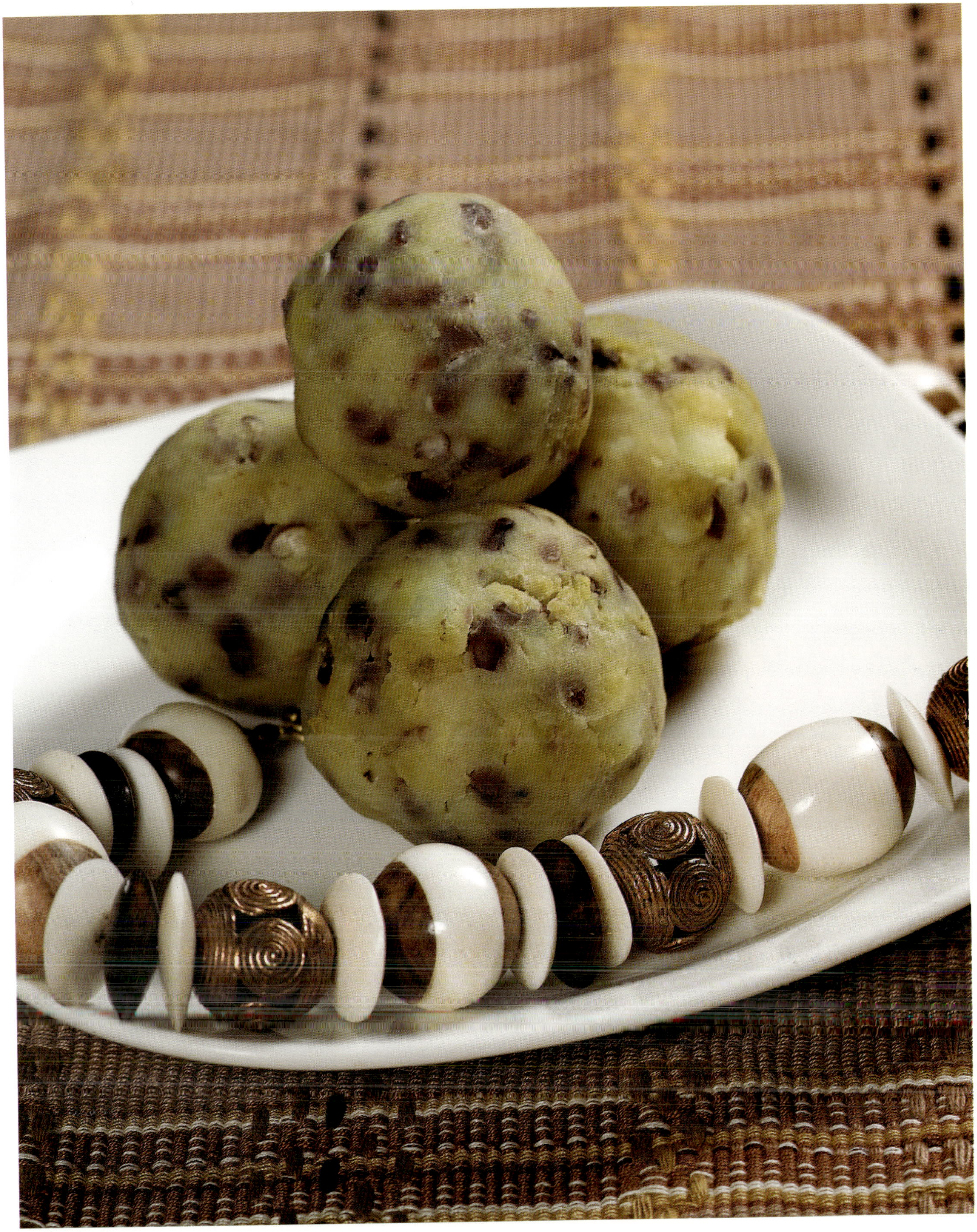

MERU

Marigo

Ingredients

8 green bananas, cut into 1 inch lengths
20 potatoes, quartered
1 kg matumbo (tripe), thinly sliced

Method

Carefully peel the bananas so that they are not bitter.
Oil your hands so that the dark sap doesn't stain.
Thoroughly wash the matumbo and then boil it in water until soft.
In the same water, add the bananas and potatoes.
Boil with some salt until cooked.
Mash to the desired consistency.

Serves 5.

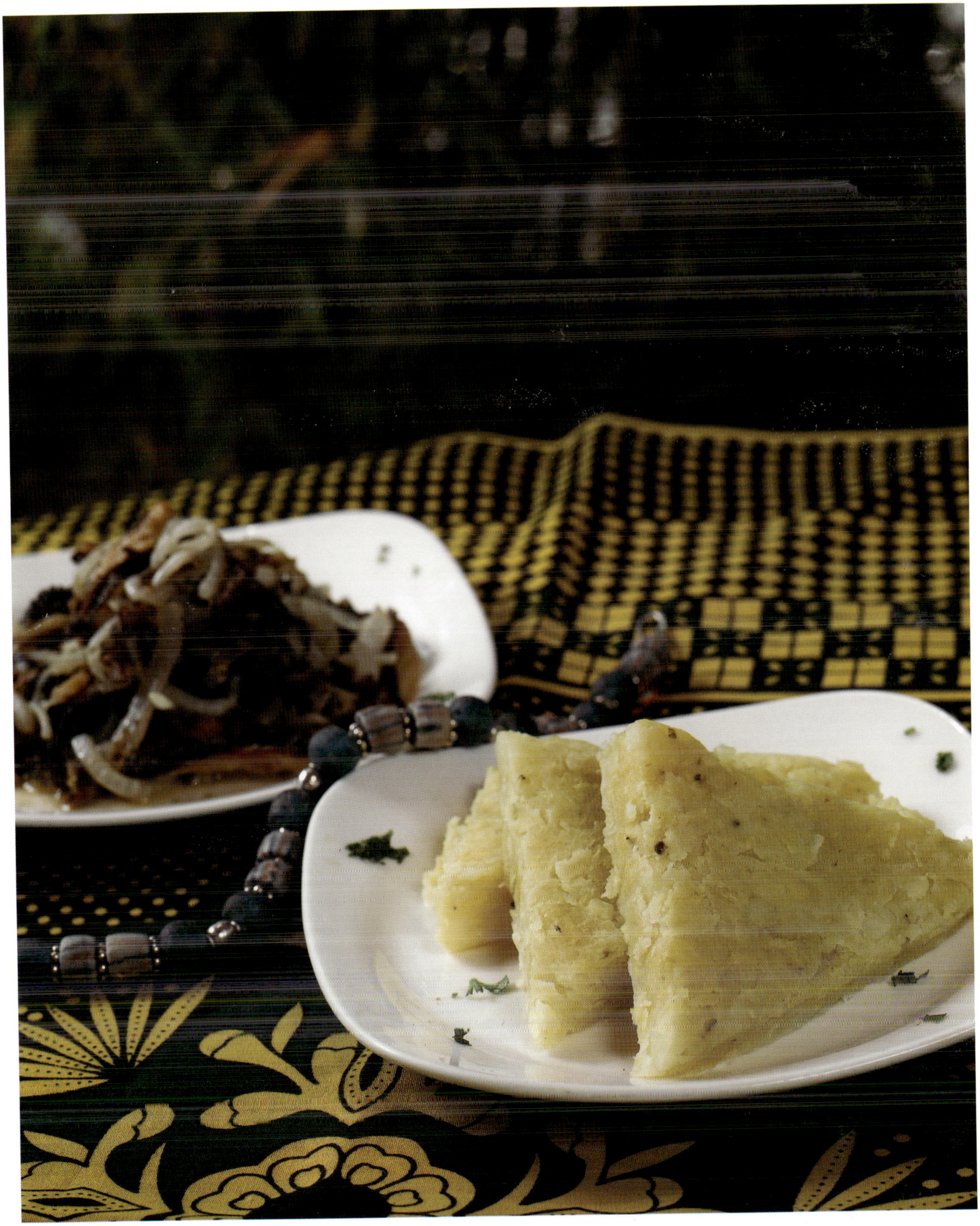

MERU

Njahi

Ingredients

3 cups njahi (dolichos labla black bean)
1 onion, chopped
2 tbsp ghee
2 tomatoes, chopped
500g goat meat, cubed
salt to taste

Method

Boil the njahi in water until it is cooked.
Fry the onion in ghee until cooked then add the tomatoes.
When cooked, add the goat meat.
When the goat meat is cooked add the njahi, salt and water to make a stew and let it simmer.

Serves 4.

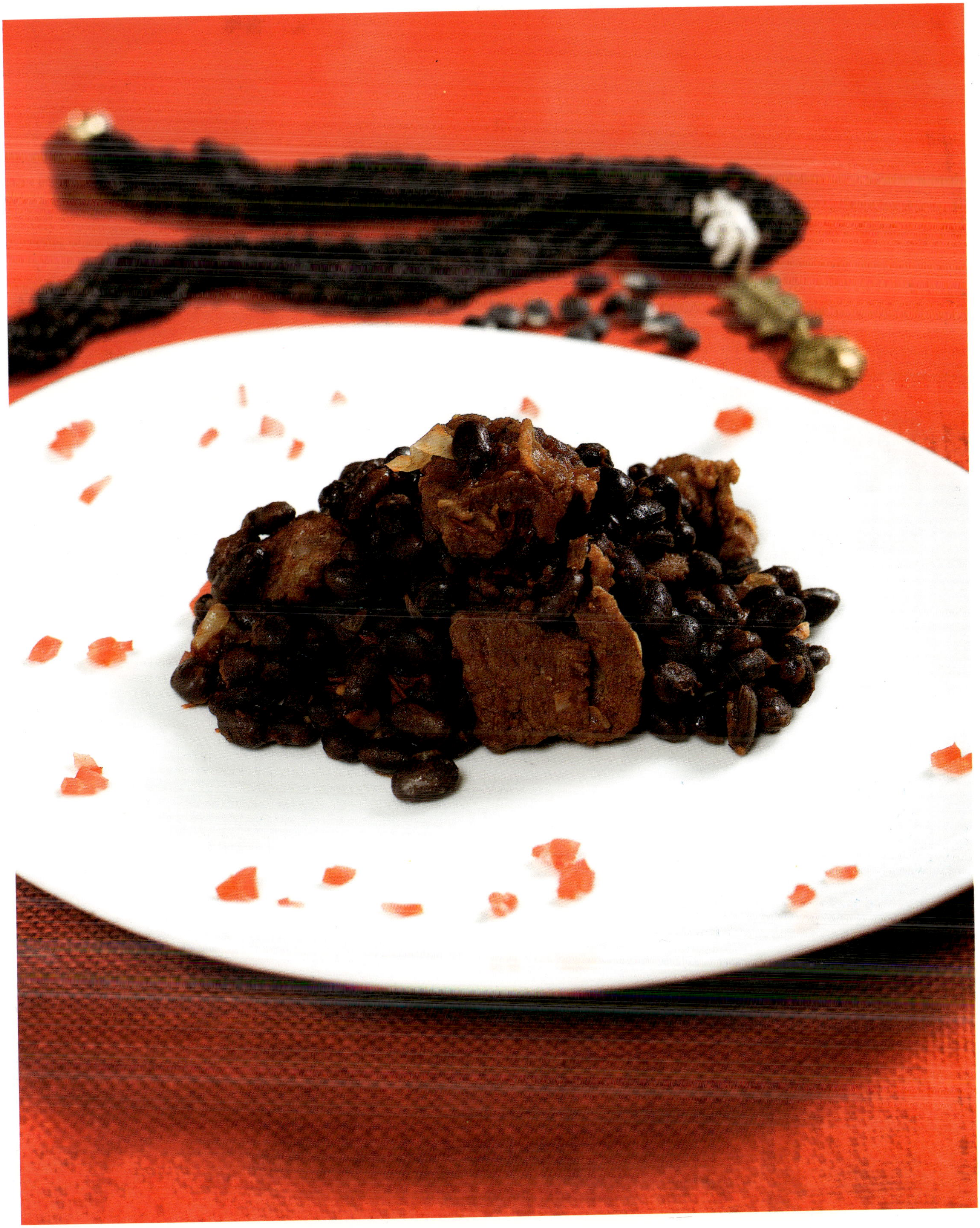

MERU

Ruguru

Ingredients

5 cups arrow root leaves, chopped
500ml water
1 cup maize meal flour
½ cup fresh milk
salt to taste

Method

Wash and then cut the arrow root leaves into the desired size.
Add water and then let it boil.
Use a traditional whisk to shred the greens further until they form a smooth liquid.
When it is cooked, add maize flour and keep whisking until cooked and slightly thickened.
Add fresh milk if desired and salt.

It is considered medicinal especially for fighting malaria

Serves 4.

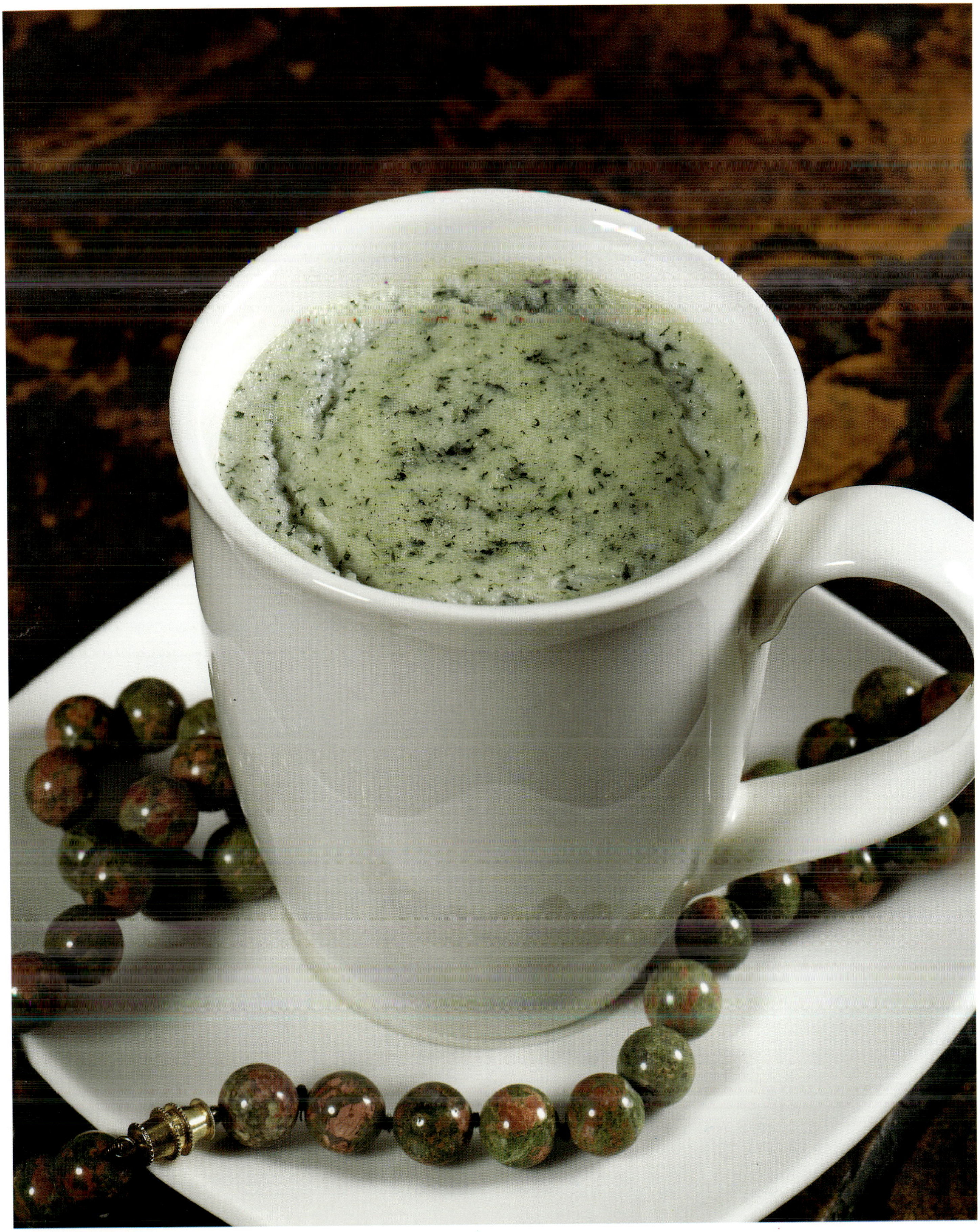

128

Mijikenda

Muhogo 132
Mchele na Kunde 134
Samaki wa Nazi 136

Boats off Lamu Island.
This island off Kenya's coast in the Indian Ocean appeals to many Europeans as well. Villas and beach property have become even more valuable following Unesco's naming of Lamu as a World Heritage Site in 2001. Many prominent Westerners have a vacation home in Africa's most expensive town.

Giriama male witchdoctor

Historically, the Mijikenda have had close interactions with the Persian, Arab, and Portuguese traders who frequented their home territory along the Kenyan coast. This interaction and subsequent intermarriage with the Arabs gave birth to the Swahili culture and language. As a result, the Swahili language – Kiswahili – bears a close lexical similarity with all dialects of the Mijikenda people. The Swahili people are a Bantu ethnic group found mainly in the coastal regions of Kenya, Tanzania and Mozambique.

Mijikenda literally means nine homes and it includes the sub communities of Giriama, Digo, Chonyi, Duruma, Jibana, Kambe, Kauma, Rabai and Ribe.

The Arabic culture has had the greatest influence in shaping Swahili traditions. Most Swahili follow a strict form of Islam and the traditional attire of a Swahili man is a long white (or beige) robe (or kaftans) known in Kiswahili as a kanzu and a small, white, rounded hat with elaborate embroidery. Swahili women dress in long black dresses called buibui, and cover their heads with a black cloth, known as a hijabu. Unlike other Kenyan communities, there are no specific rites of passage for young Swahili men and women, other than attending Madrassa (religious classes in which they study the Koran and learn the Arabic language).

Swahili weddings last several days and involve elaborate preparations, ceremonies and activities for both men and women. Only men are allowed in the mosque for the official marriage vows.

Each Mijikenda clan had their own sacred place known as kaya, a shrine for prayer, sacrifices and other religious rituals. These kayas were located deep in the forests and it was considered taboo to cut the trees and vegetation around them. The kaya elders, often members of the oldest age set, were deemed to possess supernatural powers including the ability to make rain.

For centuries the Swahili depended greatly on trade from the Indian Ocean, playing a vital role as middlemen. Swahili fishermen of today still rely on the ocean as their primary source of income.

Coconuts form a major part of the diet of the coast people but coconuts can be used for many purposes such as wine, oil, husks for floor polishing, shells for fuel, leaves for roofing, ribs for brooms, timber for building and on and on.

MIJIKENDA

Muhogo

Ingredients

1 large fresh cassava
10 bokoko (ripe bananas)
1 fresh coconut

Method

Peel and cut the cassava into pieces, then wash it and cut out the hard centre and discard.
Put the cassava in a pot with water.
Peel and wash the ripe bananas (a quantity matching the cassava pieces) and cut them into pieces.
Place these on top of the cassava.
Add 2nd and 3rd cream (coconut) to the pot together with salt.
Cover the pot and boil for 20 minutes on low heat.
Put in 1st cream mixed with salt and let it boil for another 5 minutes.
Serve with black tea.

Serves 4.

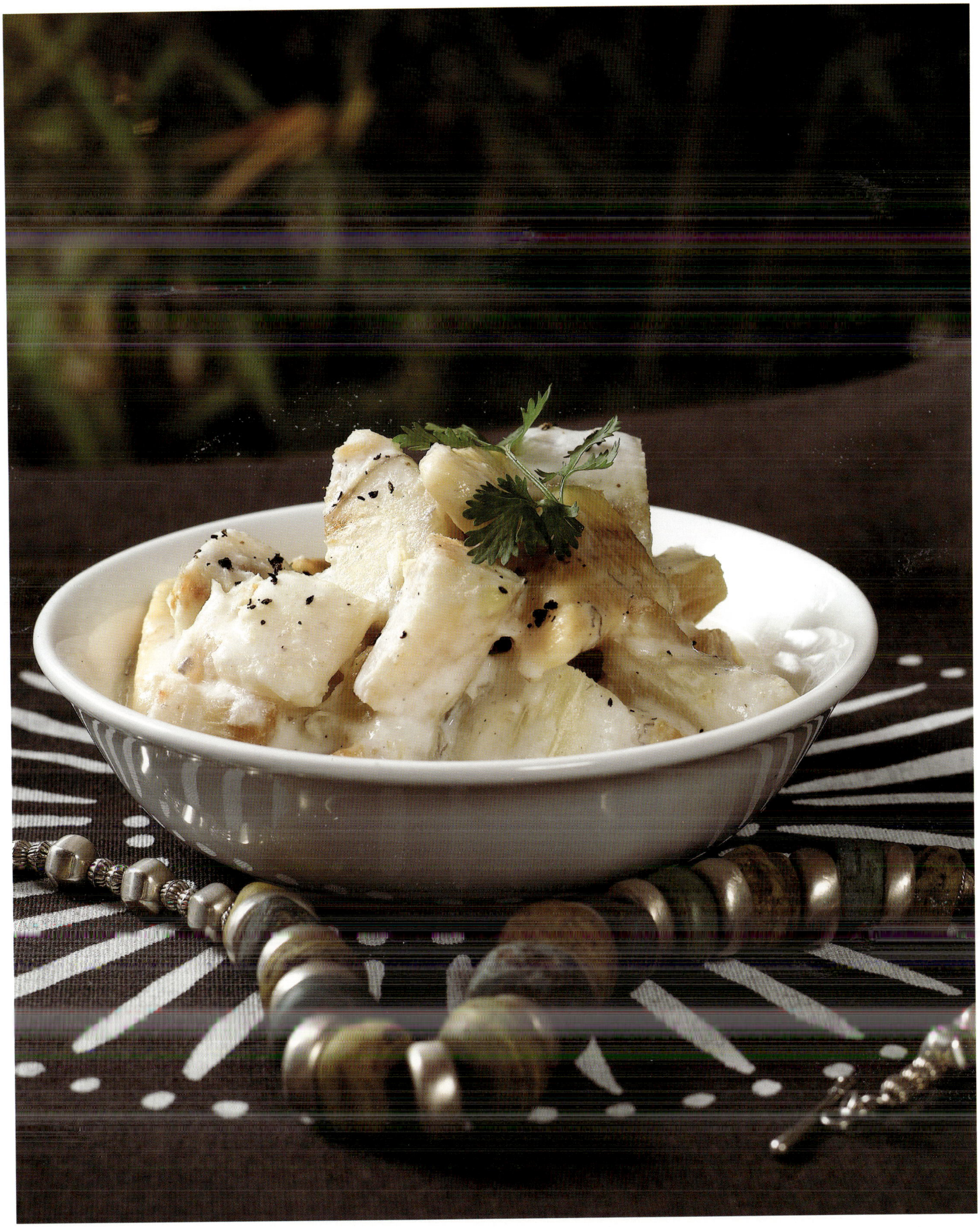

MIJIKENDA

Mchele na Kunde

Ingredients

1 cup white rice
5 cups fresh kunde leaves (cowpea leaves), shredded
1 cup coconut cream
salt to taste

Method

Boil the kunde in water for 30 minutes, or until tender.
Cook white rice with your 2nd and 3rd cream poured into the boiling salty water.
When the rice is almost cooked, add the kunde and mix lightly.
Pour the 1st cream over the top and cook on low heat until just slightly moist.

Serves 2.

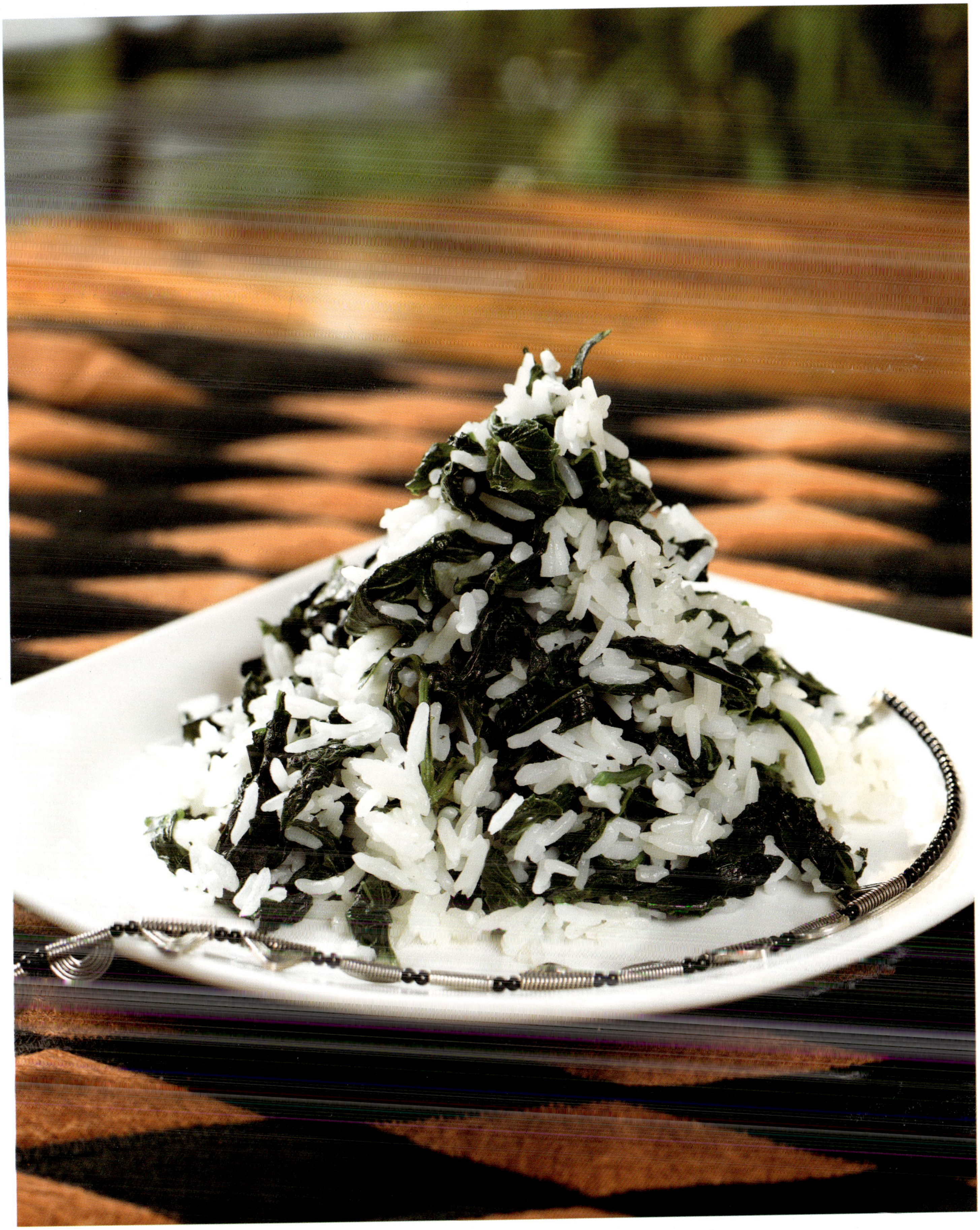

MIJIKENDA

Samaki wa Nazi

Ingredients

1 large whole fresh fish
oil for deep frying
2 onions, chopped
6 cloves of garlic, crushed
2 cups coconut cream

Method

Clean and wash the fish.
Deep fry it in hot oil for five minutes or until cooked and browned.
In a frying pan, put in the onions, garlic and 2nd and 3rd cream and let it simmer for 5 minutes, stirring continually.
Add the 1st cream and stir for another 5 minutes.
Put it aside and place the fish inside this sauce.
Serve with white rice

Serves 3.

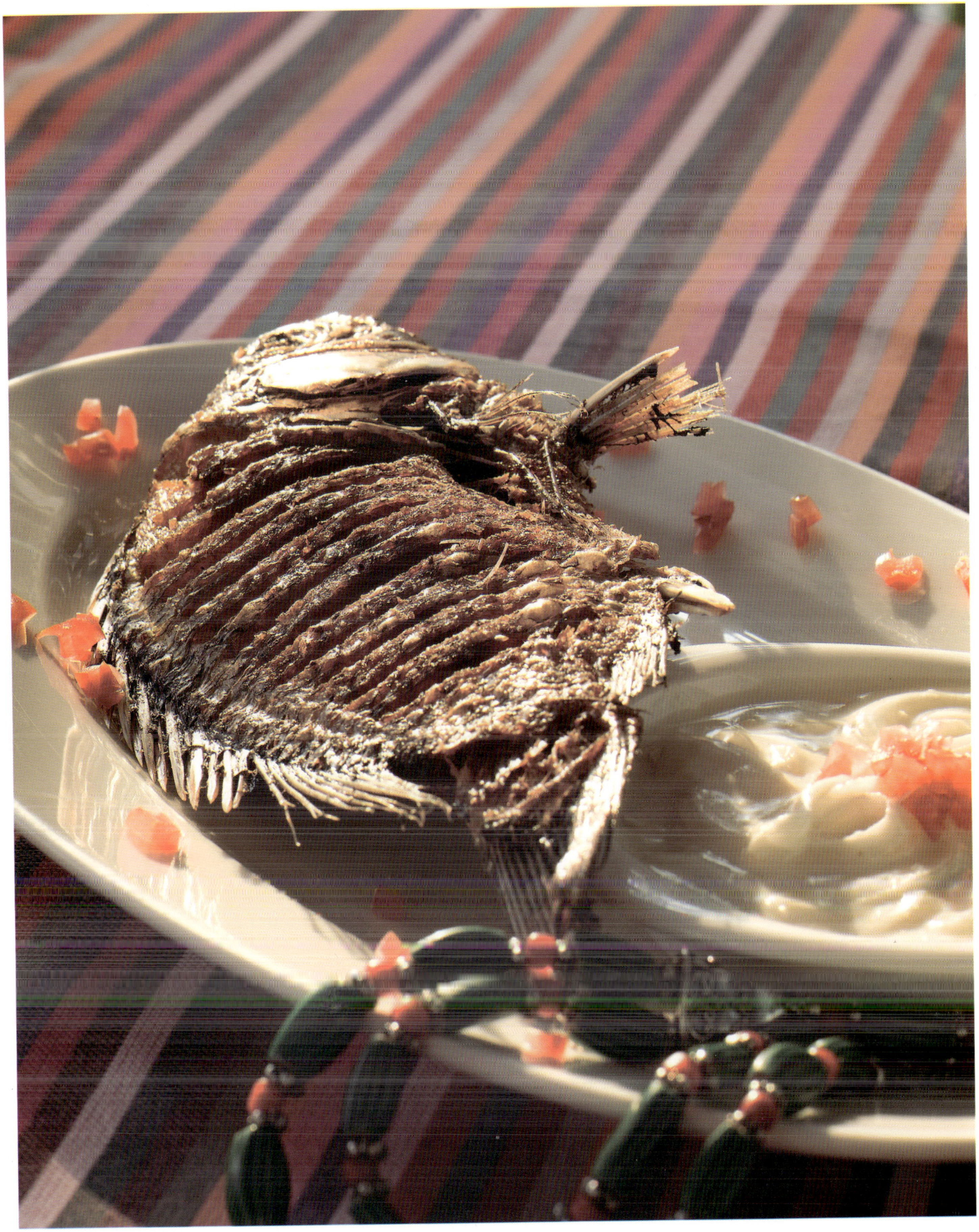

Somali

Somali Injera   142
Birris   144
Basta   146

New born calf.
Camels are kept away from villagers because the animals are considered unpredictable and likely to destroy vegetation. Shepherds live with the animals in small satellite camps. Raising camels is the traditional livelihood.

Galla man

Kenya's Somali group comes from North Eastern Province and is a Cushitic community that also resides in the neighboring Republic of Somalia and Ethiopia. All Somali are believed to have originated in the Ogaden region of Southern Ethiopia. Since the 1990s, tension and rivalry has remained high among the various clans in the Republic of Somalia as they continue to fight for land and herding areas. To date, there has been no lasting peace in the Republic of Somalia.

However, the Somali community in Kenya has maintained close historical ties with their kin in Somaliland. They have moved to the diaspora due to the conflict in Somalia and there are generations that have been born far from home yet are very committed to their culture and language. This unity makes them one of Africa's largest ethnic groups.

The Somali people practice Islam and many of their customs are derived from this religion. Somali women are known for their beauty. The Somali practice a nomadic pastoralist way of life, keeping herds of camels, sheep, cattle and goats. Nomads have few possessions and each item has practical uses such as cooking utensils, storage boxes, stools, woven mats and water bags.

In contrast with their rustic abodes, their carved headrests and woven artifacts are unmatched in careful detail and quality. The Somali are used to life in the desert and become lifelong companions with their camels. Although they come from drought prone regions of Kenya, Somalis have very interesting recipes, pasta being one of their staple dishes as they were occupied by Italy in the 1940s.

In the desert, Somali's rely heavily on camels for transport, meat and milk. Camels are amazing animals and their name means 'beauty' in Arabic. A camel hump does not store water, like most people think, it stores fat, lessening heat trapping insulation around the rest of the body. One reason camels can go long periods without water is the shape of their red blood cells. These are oval so will flow when they are dehydrated rather than clumping as ours do. The camel is the only mammal to have red blood cells. Camels can drink up to 160 litres of water in one go. Ageing camels may be slaughtered for their meat, especially when guests are expected for a celebration, and the fatty camel's hump is considered a delicacy.

SOMALI

Somali Injera

Ingredients

2 cups rice flour
1 cup wheat flour
1 cup water
sugar
salt
yeast

Method

Mix your ingredients with a little water until there are no lumps and you have a fine paste of porridge consistency.
Let it stand for three or four days until fermented.
Heat a little oil in a pan and ladle your mixture using the Moqa (spoon with a hole in the middle so you spread the batter round and round until the pan is filled with a thin layer that is thinner than a chapatti).
Sprinkle the anjera with water.
Cover the pan completely for 3 minutes.
Cook on one side only.
A variation to it is to add eggs into the mixture and fry on both sides.

Serves 4.

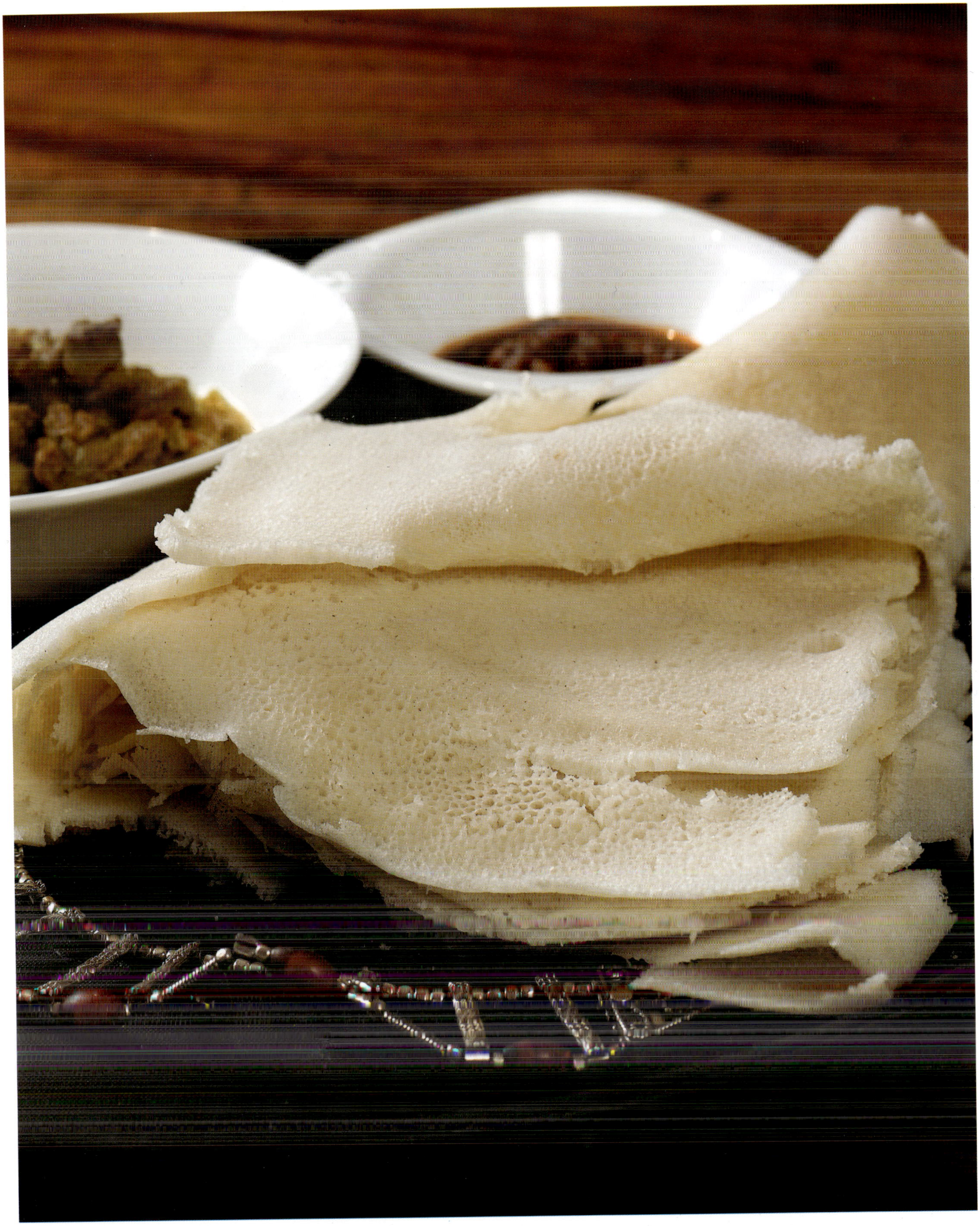

SOMALI

Birris

Ingredients

2 cups white rice
1 kg camel meat, cubed
3 tomatoes, chopped
2 tbsp tomato paste
6 potatoes, quartered
2 green pepper, chopped

4 tbsp pilau masala
2 onions, chopped
2 tbsp camel fat
large fresh ginger, crushed
salt to taste

Method

Boil your meat for 10 minutes or until tender.
Fry your onions, tomatoes, tomato paste, ginger, potatoes, green pepper and spices.
Add meat and mix into the sauce.
Put in water as per your required quantities and let it boil.
Add rice and stir the pot carefully starting with the centre and putting the spoon at the bottom of the pot and moving outwards.
When the water is almost dry, pour the camel fat on top and stir it.
Reduce heat and cover until it dries (recommend that you cover the pot with hot coal).

Serves 4.

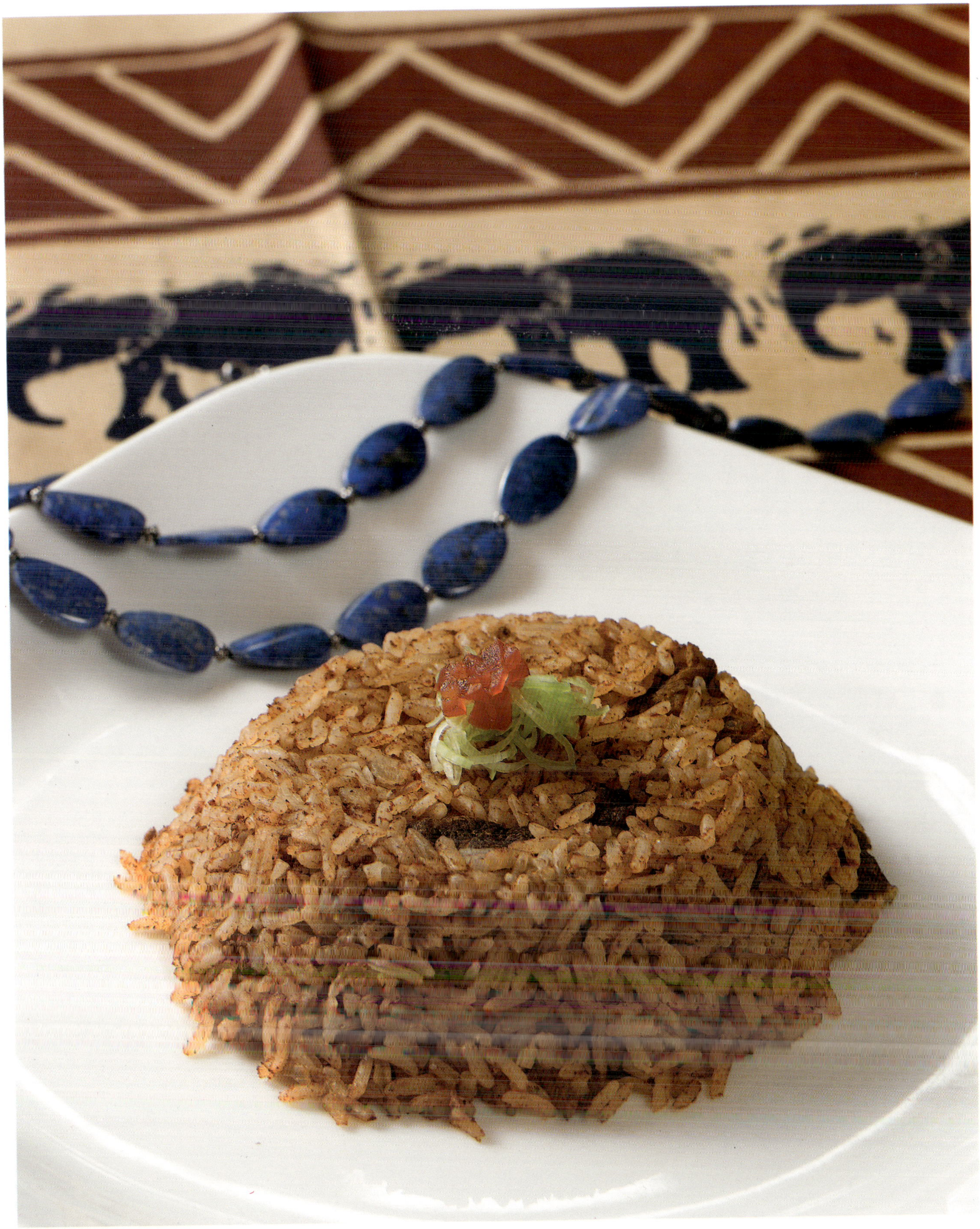

SOMALI

Basta

Ingredients

500g spaghetti
1kg camel steak, cubed
4 tbsp for shallow frying
1 onion, chopped
150g green mabenda (okra)
1 cup carrots, chopped

2 tbsp spices of your choice
2 potatoes, quartered
2 cups raw mangoes, chopped
tamarind

Method

Boil your steak for 10 minutes or until it's tender.
In another pot, fry the onions, tomatoes, raw mango, tamarind, green mabenda, potatoes and carrots.
Put in your steak and mix in with its liquid until you have a thick sauce.
Allow to cook.
Boil your pasta in water and a little oil and salt.
Drain the water, then put this water aside to use in your stew.
Run the spaghetti under cold water and put it back in the pan and stir in oil.
Pour the sauce on top of the pasta and serve.
Eat with your hands!

Serves 4.

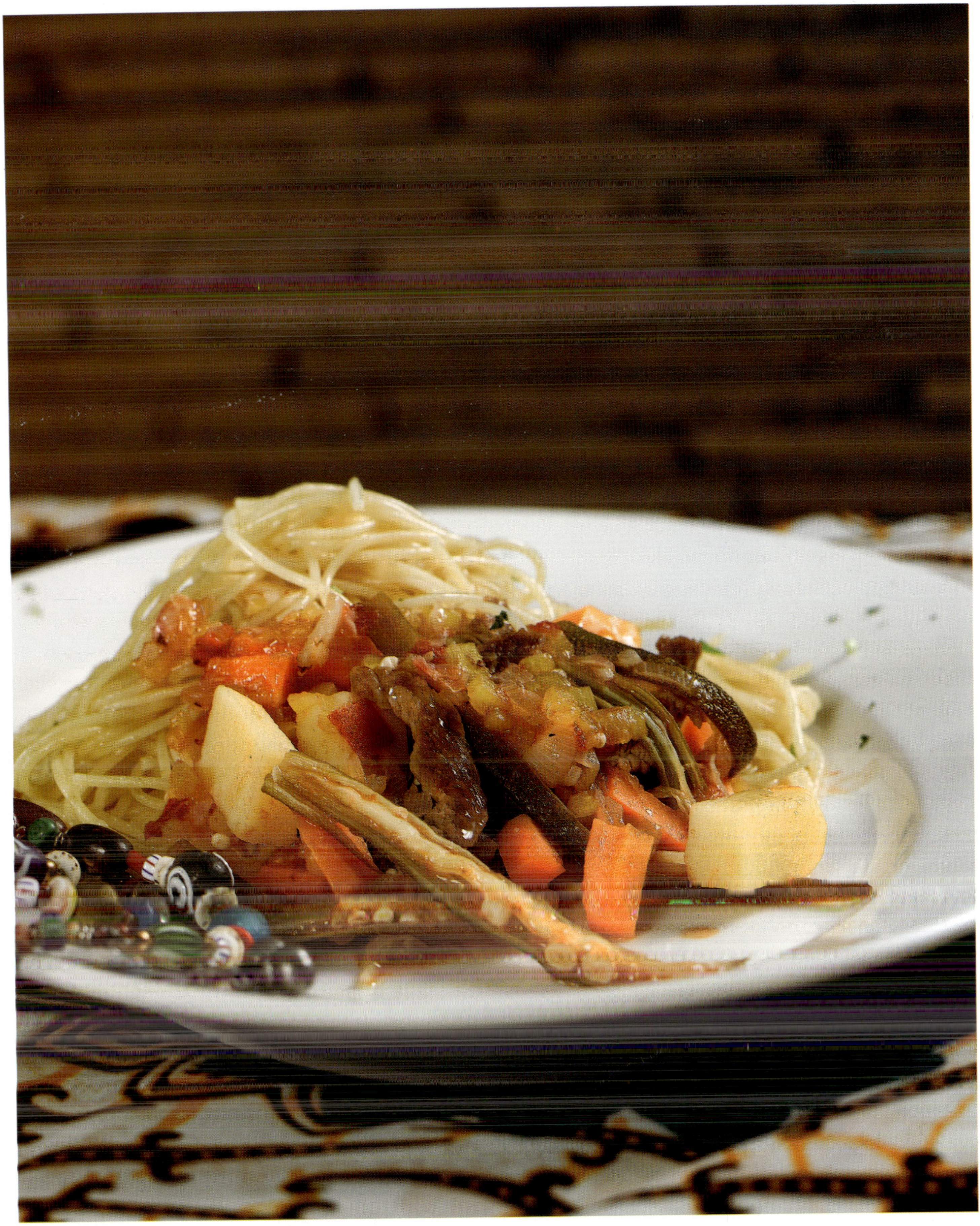

148

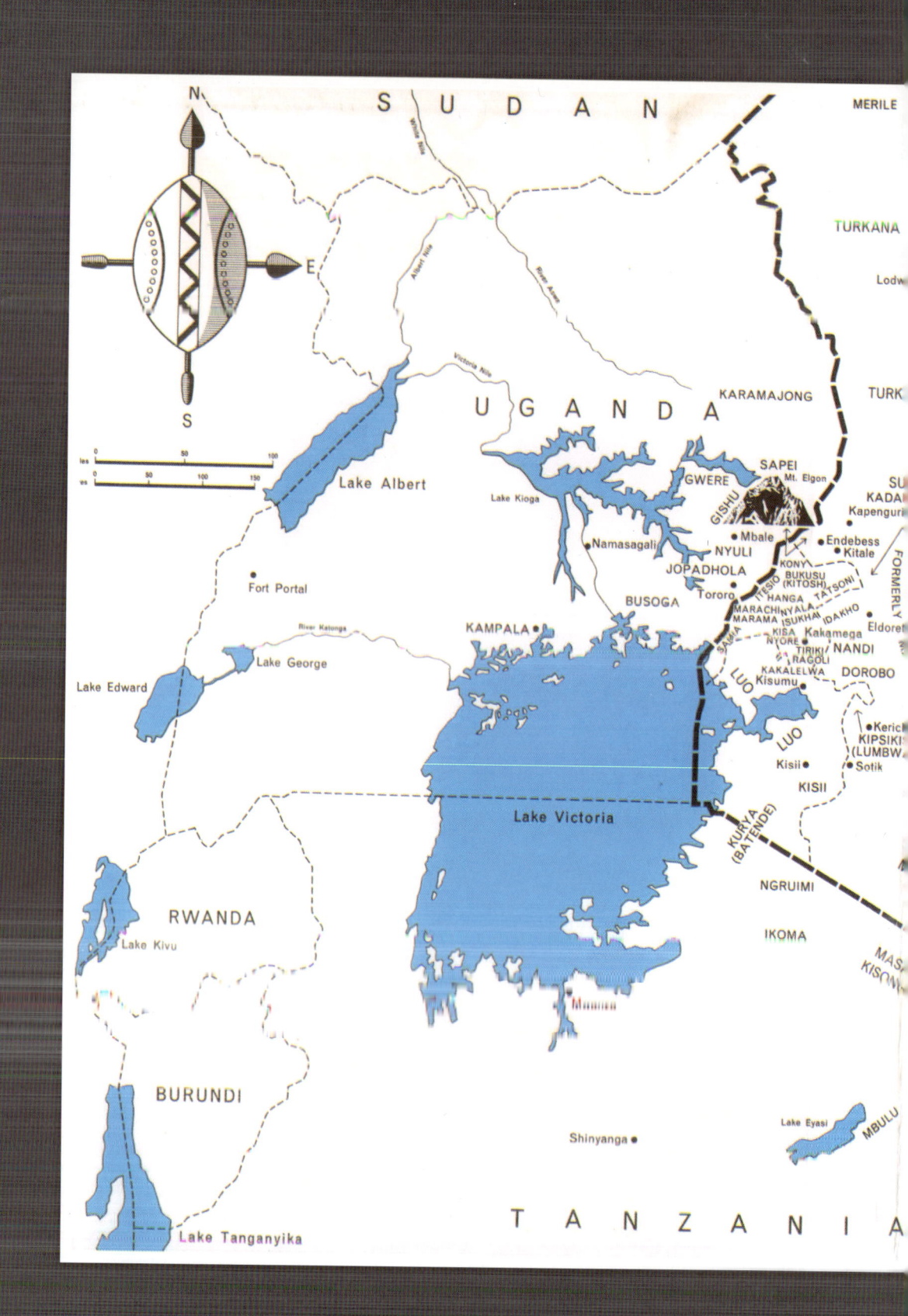

Joy Adamson map courtesy of "The Peoples of Kenya" 1967

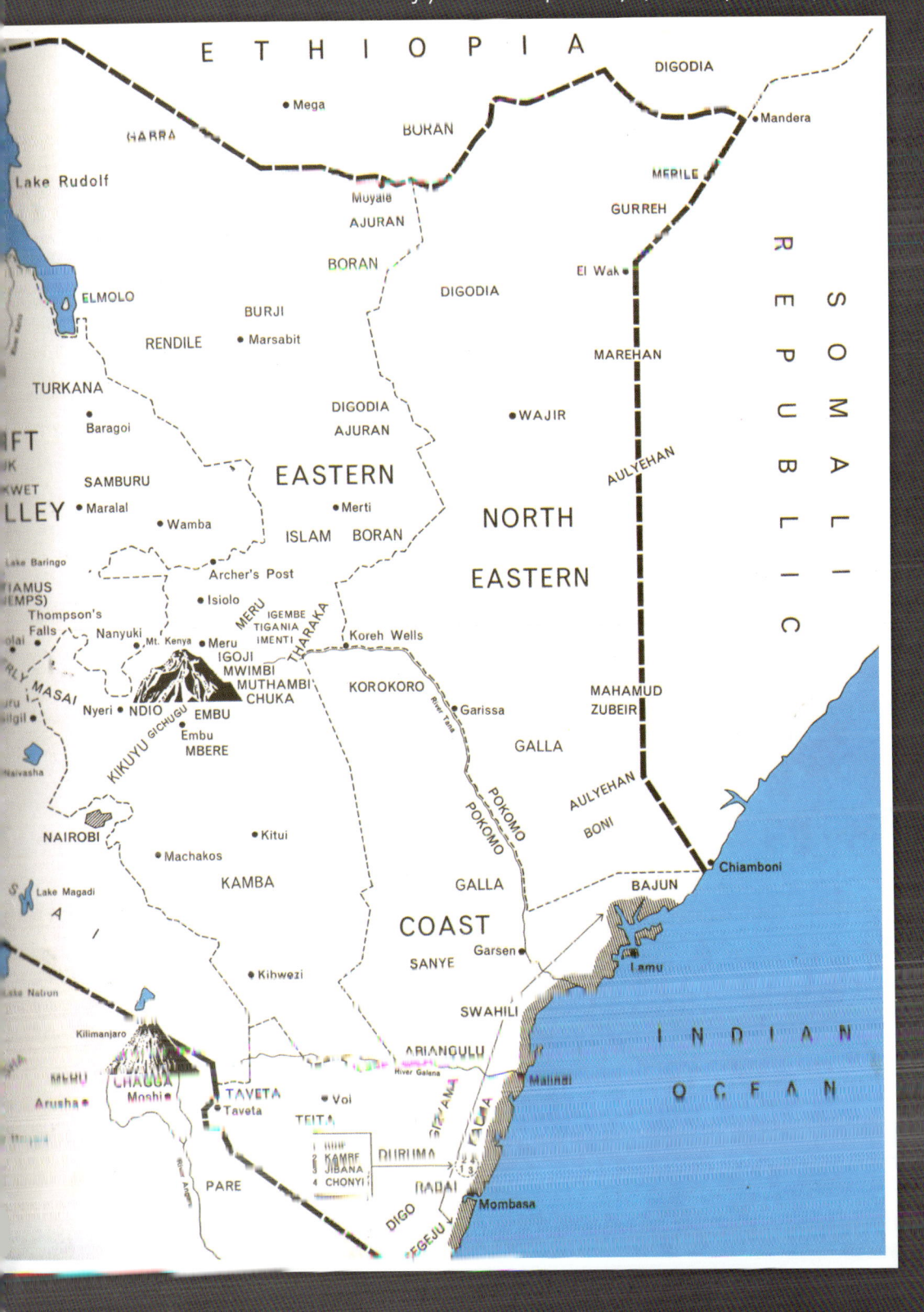

104	Aliya
98	Aluru
14	Anshiri
146	Basta
90	Bilenje
144	Birris
38	Black Lentil Curry
46	Boinnet
36	Chilli Paneer Pasanda
24	Fish & Chips
16	Foon
56	Kinaa
18	Koche Balls
48	Magrek
122	Marigo
34	Masala Chicken
134	Mchele na kunde
88	Mrenda
132	Muhogo
64	Mukimo wa Miinji
120	Muree
114	Mururi
44	Mushebebit
58	Muthokoi
66	Ngondu
54	Ngunza Kutu
124	Njahi
74	Obukima Bwobore
112	Ole Naotho
80	Omugaye
76	Omutwe we Mburi
102	Oodol
110	Rongera
126	Ruguru
78	Sagaa
136	Samulu wa Maai
92	Sikhinga
142	Somali Anjera
28	Steak & Kidney Pie
100	Sukuma Osuga Mix
26	Toad in the Hole
86	Tsiswa
68	Ucuru wa Kugagatia

Index

6